MW00528669

7 BEHAVIOURS TO EMPOWER YOU TO PUSH
THE PENDULUM TOWARDS INCLUSION AT WORK

THE ART OF ACTIVE ALLYSHIP

Explore Why Cookie Cutters Should Stay in the Kitchen Drawer

POORNIMA LUTHRA

Author of *Diversifying Diversity*

FOREWORD BY RUCHIKA TULSHYAN
Author of *Inclusion on Purpose*

For

My husband Tanuj -
my partner in life, love and intellectual conversations.

My children, Rohan and Tejas,
who are at the heart of everything I do.

My parents,
*who instilled in me a quest to expand, expand, expand
my circles of positive influence.*

The Art of Active Allyship

1st edition, November 2022
Copyright © Poornima Luthra

Author: Poornima Luthra
Book coach: Malene Bendtsen (www.malenebendtsen.com)
Editor: Dina Honour (www.dinahonour.com)
Book layout: Diren Yardimli
Cover design: Diren Yardimli

ISBN Hardback: 978-87-972903-2-3

To continue your journey as an active ally of inclusion, please visit:
artofactiveallyship.com
diversifyingdiversity.com
talented.dk

CONTENTS

Foreword 11

Author's Note 15

Introduction..21

Allyship in a Nutshell 31

The 7 Active Allyship Behaviours...53

   1 **Deep Curiosity**...55

   2 **Honest Introspection** 87

   3 **Humble Acknowledgement** 119

   4 **Empathetic Engagement**... 147

   5 **Authentic Conversations**... 191

   6 **Vulnerable Interactions**.. 215

   7 **Courageous Responsibilities**....................................... 243

Final Thoughts... 277

Acknowledgements.. 281

About the Author 283

Glossary of DEI Terms... 285

Recommended Sources 289

Endnotes.. 291

A NOTE ABOUT THE PERSONAL NARRATIVES FEATURED IN THIS BOOK

The truth is that our experiences of the workplace are not equal. To achieve true and lasting inclusion in the workplace we must be open to that truth, and open to the lived experiences of others. We must walk in their shoes. The personal narratives featured in this book are a way for us to do that. These first-hand experiences are an important way for us to connect and to understand the way that biases and discrimination affect others, seen through the eyes of those who have experienced them. Reading and reflecting upon these experiences is an essential part of engaging in the behaviours that enable us to be active allies, the very behaviours laid out in this book. They are a sounding board for us to be able to identify our own biases. As you read these deeply personal stories, remember to engage honestly and empathetically.

The narratives featured in this book are the contributors' own, have been approved for publication, and have only been edited for clarity. Every effort has been made through the editorial process to retain each contributors' own unique and authentic voice as they share their stories of bias and discrimination arising from their intersectional identities, and offer suggestions for active allyship.

For their courage and openness, I am deeply grateful to each of them. I hope that you will feel inspired by their stories, the way I have.

I hope you will take a moment to walk in their shoes.

FOREWORD

By Ruchika Tulshyan

Early in my career, I was in a meeting and my senior manager kept referring to me as a "Roo-sheek-ah." He said it again and again, proudly sharing how I was leading a new project on his team. It was great to have my work recognized.

The only problem is, my name is pronounced "Roo-cheek-ah." And I had been on his team for over 6 months.

While I corrected his pronunciation in our one-on-one meetings, I felt too embarrassed and unsafe as a junior woman of color to correct him in that larger meeting. So swallowing my shame, I tried to ignore it. I worked hard to rearrange my face each time so that no one could see the slight cringe on my face every time he mispronounced my name.

When I looked around the table at that meeting, I was surprised to see several coworkers cringing when he mispronounced my name. I thought no one else noticed, but it was clear that many did.

All my colleagues at that meeting were white, like him, and many were male. But no one corrected him.

After the meeting, a colleague by the name of John came up to me and said:

"Wow, he really butchered your name, huh? Too bad! Anyway, I just want you to know that I'm an ally and I'd never do that, Ruchika." He pronounced my name correctly. But what he said was incorrect.

He was not an ally.

I looked at my colleague and said, "you're not an ally." I don't know where the words or courage came from, certainly not at that time so early in my career. In those days, I was just grateful to be in the room and had never stood up for myself in any meaningful way. But I was fed up and I couldn't take it any more.

He snorted: "Of course I am an ally. Did you not just hear me say your name correctly?"

I responded calmly: "An ally is not who you are, it's what you do. You did not ally with me when you recognized the mispronunciation but chose not to say anything."

It's been over a decade, but I still recall every detail of that conversation.

I understood why John called himself an ally. I've often called myself an ally in my life; I studied journalism in an effort to give voice to those who had been silenced. I thought I was being an ally every time I covered a story about a community that had been misrepresented or left out by the media.

Here's the thing though: ally is a verb, not a noun. So perhaps while I was practicing allyship in some moments, I can't call myself an ally.

In reality, nobody should call themselves an ally. As I said all those years ago, an ally is not who you are, it's what you do.

John hadn't practiced active allyship in that meeting–if he did, he would have interrupted my boss at some point and said calmly, "her name is pronounced Roo-Cheek-ah." It didn't have to turn into a big ordeal (and I would have been so embarrassed if it did!) but a quick, calm intervention when it mattered most would have made me feel welcome and valued. And hopefully ensured that my boss would learn from that interaction.

Research shows that often the more privilege we have, the less empathy we have for others who don't share the same identities as us. But if my boss heard from John––someone with similar privilege and identities as him––that he was mispronouncing my name, there's a higher chance that he would have corrected himself going forward.

John also had a lot less to lose than I did in correcting my boss's pronunciation of my name. John is a white man and although he was junior to my boss, he had a cordial relationship with him and the two often went to lunch together.

The challenge with practicing allyship in a group setting, or what social psychologists call the "bystander effect" is that around others, we often think it's another person's responsibility to pipe up and disrupt biased, bullying, toxic or even violent behavior. In fact, the larger the group, the less likely any one individual will step in to stop the biased or bad behavior.

And that is precisely why we have made paltry progress in creating inclusive, equitable workplaces where everyone can truly belong. For too long, we've deflected responsibility and over-indexed on our "good intentions" and that we are an "ally."

But, meaningful change means making ourselves uncomfortable. Often, it means giving up something–whether it's the comfort of our peers or bosses, an opportunity, or even coming off as "the disruptor." Active allyship requires action.

This is why Dr. Poornima Luthra's book is so urgent.

First, we need to recognize which stage of allyship we are currently in. Then, we must familiarize ourselves with the seven allyship behaviors. As Poornima so eloquently and brilliantly writes: "To develop this depth of understanding, we need to be curious. We need to build our knowledge base about issues in the area of diversity, equity and inclusion. We need to understand where biases and discrimination come from. We need to listen with curiosity, not simply to respond, but to learn from the experiences of bias and discrimination from those from under-represented, marginalised and discriminated groups. Not knowing the full extent of the biases that exist means that we are unable to address them."

This work requires us to "see" what is invisible. To name what might feel unspeakable. And to take courageous actions that we may have never had to demonstrate before, or seen demonstrated by our peers or leaders.

But that is where meaningful change begins. With one person. In one moment. It can begin with you.

Read this book not because you have a box to check or want a badge to validate all that you've already done. Read this book because you know this is a lifelong journey. You will likely never be done. I'm certainly not. But I know for sure that the only way we can create a world where everyone has a chance to fully participate, to show up bringing their authentic selves to the workplace, is one where we each walk towards bravery and action. Where, even if we're the first to practice allyship, we keep on doing it because it's the right and courageous thing to do.

Poornima has written a courageous manifesto that lays out the art and science of active allyship. As a woman of color born outside a western country, who works with many leaders who want to do the right thing, I'm delighted that this book exists as a guide for all leaders.

May you find in it, like I did, inspiration, courage and compassion. In hard moments, I come back to the words of Archbishop Desmond Tutu: "'If you are neutral in situations of injustice, you have chosen the side of the oppressor."

I hope you'll always choose to stand up against injustice.

Together, we can, and will change the world through practicing active allyship.

AUTHOR'S NOTE

What can I do?

It's a question that comes up time and time again in my interactions with employees, managers and leaders of companies across the world.

What can I do?

Diversity, Equity and Inclusion (DEI) are increasingly becoming one of the cornerstones of companies' talent strategies. Rightfully so, and long past time. So far, companies have been focused on justifying DEI through the business case, developing their DEI strategy and roadmap, and building the required structures and systems to support that strategy. Despite all these efforts, here we are here in 2022 where inequalities in our workplaces - and society - are still rampant. What is missing and how do we move the pendulum further and faster towards inclusive environments for all?

Here is the thing - inclusion at work is not experienced through strategies and roadmaps. It is experienced in our day-to-day interactions with others - with our colleagues, managers and leaders. This means that we cannot move the pendulum without each of us seeing ourselves as key enablers of inclusive workplaces - workplaces where everyone feels valued, respected, appreciated and feels a sense of belonging. We need every employee to see their role in this, and we need everybody to make efforts to act in a way that nurtures inclusive environments. This is what is currently missing - we don't have everybody on board, and even for those who are on board, the question remains - *what can I do?*

Over many years of working with employees, managers and leaders, I believe that what we need to make our workplaces truly inclusive is active allyship comprising of a clear set of practical behaviours that we can embed into our day-to-day working lives. To address this need, I present to you 7 behaviours in The Art of Active Allyship. The content presented in this book has been tested with thousands of employees, leaders and audiences over the past three years across more than 25 global companies through keynotes, talks and workshops. Using a continuous iterative process, improvements to the seven behaviours and their tools have been made during this period.

These seven behaviours provide concrete actions that we can all engage in to ensure that we are being inclusive for diverse colleagues in our workplaces. You won't need any fancy equipment, a facilitator, DEI coach or trainer. The behaviours here are not dependent on a company's DEI strategy but are certainly complimentary to it. We all have a choice in every interaction we have with others at work - to do what is inclusive or not. My hope is that these seven behaviours will provide you with all you need to show up every day in all workplace circumstances to be an active ally and do the inclusive thing.

On a recent visit to one of my favourite art museums - the Louisiana Museum of Modern Art in Denmark - I found myself reflecting on the connection between the process of becoming an active ally and evolving as an artist. Hence the title of this book - *the art* of active allyship. As I explored the work of the particular artist on display at that time, it was evident that the artist's work was continuously evolving;

continuously progressing; very much like allyship. To evolve as an artist requires practice and discipline alongside engaging in frequent and consistent behaviours to continuously develop one's technique and skill. I also found myself seeing the art in front of me as a reflection of the artist's thoughts, feelings and beliefs. As I stared into an abstract painting, it hit me - if we want our actions to be inclusive in the canvas of our workplaces, we first need to introspect and put in effort to ensure that our thoughts, feelings and beliefs are inclusive. To do this, an artist needs tools. After all, one cannot be a painter without brushes or a sculptor without a hammer. The seven behaviours in this book include the tools for us to be an active ally.

When writing this book, I was also keen to give you, the reader, an opportunity to hear what active allyship can look and feel like directly from individuals who have experienced intersectional biases and discrimination. I am a firm believer in the power of narratives. Human relationships are built upon the sharing of stories within and across generations. These personal narratives or stories are needed in workplaces for us to share perspectives, negotiate, and create empathy. DEI is not just a rational issue; it is a deeply emotive one. While for some of us the rational drivers for being more inclusive are enough, for the vast majority of us, it is the emotive side that gets us to sway towards doing more to be inclusive to others. The personal narratives shared here by these amazing individuals are powerful; they bring the seven behaviours to life. I hope their stories will move you as they have moved me. I hope they will inspire you to be an active ally just as they have inspired me. I am grateful for their courage to share their stories so that we can all do better.

Before we begin, a word of caution. The journey towards active allyship will involve many moments of discomfort. This discomfort is natural, expected and shows your commitment to this process. It is in this discomfort that we learn the most about ourselves and how we interact with others. Getting uncomfortable and wriggling in your seat are exactly where I would like you to be. As I often tell my clients, if you aren't feeling even slightly uncomfortable then I haven't done my job well. I am not here to reassure you that you are already doing the right things. I am here to push you to do more. Becoming an active ally requires us to take a deep hard look at ourselves, question the biases we hold, inquire where they come from and reflect on what we can do differently. This is hard, challenging even. It is uncomfortable. It can be uneasy. But it is essential to moving forward.

In recent years, I have personally been at the receiving end of active allyship. I have had active allies advocate for me, recommend me for career progression opportunities, and stand up for me by addressing biases and discrimination against me. I have experienced the positive and very profound impact it can have on someone, on a deeply personal level. Many of these allies have experienced the magic of active allyship themselves and are paying it forward by showing up every day to be an active ally for others. These active allies in my life are my inspiration.

I am a realistic optimist. I believe that inclusion happens in day-to-day actions. Sure, we need the occasional grand gesture, but what we really need are frequent and consistent allyship behaviours by all involved. I also believe in the positive intent of people. I believe that the vast majority of people want to do better; they want to be a part of nurturing inclusion. In the words of Nigerian author Chimamanda Ngozi Adichie: "Culture does not make people. People make culture".[1] If we desire inclusive cultures, empowering us all to nurture that culture is the key. To feel empowered, we need to know what to do.

This book is for anyone who works with others in a company, organisation or institution, regardless of position, role or responsibilities. We need talent from both represented and under-represented groups to be active allies. We need those who are privileged to be active allies, and we also need those who have experienced biases and discrimination them-selves to be active allies to others like them, and to other under-repre-sented, marginalised and discriminated groups that they are not a part of. We can only achieve inclusive workplaces for all when everyone in our workplaces recognises their individual role in being an active ally, and acts to co-nurture an inclusive culture. While this book focuses on the workplace context, my hope is that you will feel motivated to be inclusive outside the workplace as well.

If you are wondering - who should I be an active ally *to*, the answer is simple - to anyone who is from an under-represented, marginalised and discriminated group. If you already consider yourself an ally, ask yourself how you can be an even better ally. If you are an active ally to women, ask yourself if you are being an ally to *all* women, across all intersectional identities (for example, women of colour, disabled women, neurodiverse women, trans-women, lesbian women, mothers, etc.). And finally, ask how you can be an active ally to other identities beyond the ones you are comfortable being an ally to. If you aren't sure of the answer to the last question, then this book will help you to expand your sphere of active allyship.

I don't promise that the journey to nurturing inclusion will be easy. In fact, I will, in the spirit of radical honesty, say that it will be hard. But my hope is that this book will be your companion; the "hand" holding you along the way. So every time you feel like it is too much, know that you are not alone. Be kind to yourself and others.

I believe that we sit at a unique point in human history - to do better for all and not just some. Are you ready to learn the art of active allyship?

This is me paying it forward.

Poornima

INTRODUCTION

"Be the change you want to see in the world."
MAHATMA GANDHI, Indian lawyer,
anti-colonial nationalist and political ethicist

It is the year 2022, and a good time to take stock of the Diversity, Equity and Inclusion (DEI) efforts in our workplaces. If we think of DEI as a pendulum, for most of history it has been stuck in one position. There has been movement thanks to equal opportunity laws and anti-discrimination policies, but the pendulum remains fixed. To reach a point of true inclusion, where everyone feels respected, valued, and a sense of belonging, the pendulum must shift away from the inequality that exists today towards greater inclusion.

Where are we now?

You will be hard-pressed to find an organisation that does not have a focus on DEI right now. When we look at the DEI journey of organisations, we observe some common patterns emerging. To date, DEI efforts have focused on four key areas:

- Establishing the business case for DEI.
- Developing the DEI vision and strategy.
- Establishing the supporting systems and structures.
- Making efforts to address systemic biases.

While the order may vary slightly across companies, components of the above key pillars are present in most.

In recent months, I have heard an increasing number of CEOs and CHROs share their thoughts on the need to move beyond the business case of DEI towards actual cultural transformation. The companies that these leaders helm all have a clear DEI vision and strategy. They have a set of company values that incorporate the word inclusion, and even a roadmap to guide them, focusing on awareness building and reviewing systems and processes. While all of this is great progress, the leaders of these companies recognise that they are certainly not where we would like to be. They are concerned - they seem to be doing all the right things but the pendulum still won't budge - or when it does, does so too slowly.

When it comes to many other organisational transformation efforts such as restructuring, digital transformation and even the green transition, having a clear vision, strategy, leadership support and champions often gets the ball rolling and enables change. However, for DEI, while these ingredients are vital, they are simply not enough. This is as much as we need the most junior person in the company to be inclusive. If we want to see real change and progress in DEI and have inclusive workplaces for all, we need everyone to recognise their role in making this happen. We need every employee to be inclusive in meetings, when getting coffee with colleagues and at lunch. Inclusion requires all hands-on-deck,

Establish the business case for DEI

Conduct a DEI audit to understand the current status and identify areas of improvement

Build awareness of the need for DEI in the organisation

Develop the DEI vision and strategy

Embed DEI in the company's talent strategy

Collect data and set targets

Develop a supporting road map

Include DEI in ESG reporting

Establish supporting systems and structures

Hire key DEI leadership champions

Establish a dedicated and resourced team to address DEI

Establish DEI councils / task forces / sounding boards

Set up Employee Resource groups (ERGs)

Conduct DEI, bias awareness and inclusive leadership training

Address systemic biases

Review recruitment and selection processes

Address pay gaps, parental leave, and childcare options

Review how inclusive products and services are to diverse customers

Review marketing campaigns

Cultural transformation through personal action

Focus on individual action – allyship - to nurture inclusion

Review progress through surveys including employee engagement surveys

Diversity, Equity & Inclusion (DEI) journey of organisations

and progress towards inclusive workplaces can only be achieved when we have commitment from the vast majority of employees, such that it becomes impossible for someone not to be inclusive. Only then would we have the critical mass necessary for inclusion and inclusive cultures to flourish.

Unfortunately, we do not have everyone on board. Many of us have likely been in situations when the non-inclusive behaviour or behaviours of a single member of a team has changed the dynamics and vibe in the team. That behaviour could take the form of a joke, the use of offensive language or making a decision that is biased. Some see addressing inequality, bias and discrimination as a women's issue. Others see it as an issue for under-represented ethnic groups or the LGBTQ+ or the disabled or neurodiverse communities. Except it isn't an issue for just these groups. This is an issue that can only be addressed when individuals from represented and under-represented groups alike actively work to co-nurture inclusive cultures. This is a human issue; an issue that concerns us all.

For those thinking "but I'm not the one engaging in non-inclusive behaviours", passivity is its own form of non-inclusive behaviour. Being a bystander and letting biases and discrimination continue to exist without acting against them won't move the pendulum towards inclusion. We all have a responsibility and an individual role in enabling inclusion. This is not a time for apathy or disinterest. This is a time in human history for change and transformation - for the better - and betterment for all. We need to see ourselves as an integral part of the solution. We need everyone on board - and yet everyone is not. Why?

What is standing in the way?

In a word, fear. In the DEI space, there is plenty of fear: fear of being discriminated against, of getting things wrong, of saying the wrong things, or of feeling uncomfortable. There is sometimes fear of being misunderstood or misrepresented, of being the lone voice, of being the token hire, or even the fear of not doing anything.

Those who are well represented are scared and so are those who are under-represented, marginalised and discriminated against. I've had clients share that they feel like they are walking on eggshells, fearful of doing or saying the wrong thing. I have heard from represented group members who feel like the deck is stacked against them. They are worried about their own career opportunities in a world that seems to suddenly favour everyone but them. On the other side, I know that those from under-represented, marginalised and discriminated groups fear being seen as a diversity hire. They fear that bringing up biases and discrimination will affect how they are perceived at work and their opportunities for career progress. These fears prevent us from moving the pendulum further and faster towards nurturing inclusive workplaces for all.

I occasionally get asked: "Is there a limit to being woke and addressing injustice?". My answer: "No, there isn't, not until everyone feels seen, heard and valued for being their whole diverse selves." As long as discrimination exists, our work continues. Sometimes I am asked: "Isn't it too much when we start nit-picking everything we say and labelling it as being non-inclusive?" Change often feels overwhelming, even small changes. Suddenly it can seem as if we are treading carefully, unsure what terms to use or not use. When the slow shift from gendered terms like waitress or stewardess towards server and flight attendant occurred, the change was met with resistance. Over time, we became accustomed to them. Of course, we should not become pedantic or extremist in our approach, but we do need to do things differently - inclusively.

I also often get asked - usually by a White man - "All of this feels like 'reverse' discrimination; how is that fair? Why should I feel bad about my privilege? I didn't ask to be born this way." My response: That is discrimination, not reverse discrimination. Discrimination is discrimination; the same kind that many under-represented, marginalised and discriminated groups have experienced for centuries and continue to experience. Discrimination does not become "unacceptable" when it is against a represented group, and "acceptable" when it is against under-represented groups. It is always unacceptable. As an activist adage sums up, "When you're accustomed to privilege, equality feels like oppression."

Through this cultural transformation, it will get uncomfortable. For those belonging to a represented group, it may even seem unfair. Facing that discomfort can be daunting. We will need to sit with it, reflect and use the opportunity to empathise with others who have experienced this for far longer than we have - the Black colleague who has been overlooked for promotions time and time again; the Asian woman who has been paid less; the neurodiverse employee who does not even make it to the shortlist or the Muslim woman who is told she is not a good "fit" with the company. To correct the inequalities, inequities, and injustices, the pendulum has to swing towards inclusion. In the course of that change it will feel uncomfortable for those of us who have enjoyed being well-represented. It will need us to let go of the power over decision making, resources and opportunities that we have been hoarding. We will need to make space for others. If we can overcome this discomfort and come to terms with *letting go*, then inclusive workplaces can become a reality.

Looking ahead: What is next?

In the words of the 19th century American writer Mary Roberts Reinhart: "When knowledge comes in the door, fear and superstition fly out." I believe that we should harness the present momentum in DEI to push the pendulum further and faster towards inclusion, and the best way to do that is through know-how. The more we understand something and the more we know what to do, the less fearful we are of it. With this know-how, we need to set things right - but right for all, not just for some. If done well, it will mean more opportunities for everyone. DEI is good for business, which means growth. Growth means space for all. What we need to remind ourselves is that inclusion is not an *either/or* journey. It isn't about one group at the expense of others. Inclusion is an *and* journey. In truly inclusive workplaces, there is space for everyone.

What's clear is that nurturing inclusive cultures will not happen because of a DEI strategy, road map or systemic changes alone. We need to act and the time to act is now. We need a critical mass of people challenging the way things have been done and actively engaging. That means individuals stepping up. It isn't sufficient to simply believe in DEI, or say that you do. We are at an important juncture, and in front of us is the chance to transform our workplaces. We can help right the wrongs - the inequality, the biases, the discrimination. The seven behaviours laid out in the book will empower each of us to be active allies. Together we can make inclusion for all a reality. Together we can move the pendulum.

Making Sense of DEI: The terminology

Diversity refers to our differences and is the state of being diverse. It is based on the understanding that each person is unique and recognises that people have differences across a range of intersectional or interrelated human qualities or dimensions. *Surface-level diversity dimensions* are those that are visible and include, but are not limited to, sex, race, age, body size, or visible disabilities. *Deep-level diversity dimensions* are those that are invisible and include, but are not limited to, thinking styles, perspectives, experiences, values, and beliefs.

Inclusion is a culture, an environment where everyone is respected and appreciated as valuable members, where their voice is heard, and where they feel a sense of belonging. Unlike diversity, inclusion is more nebulous. Inclusion is made up of emotions and feelings from our lived experiences when interacting with others. We *feel* inclusion, and our interactions with others are the vehicle through which we experience inclusion. Our answers to questions in employee engagement surveys like "Do you feel included?" or "Do you feel like you belong?" are highly subjective. The very same environment can be experienced very differently by two different people. Our perceptions of inclusion are influenced by the lens through which we experience it. This lens comprises who we are, our life experiences and the social conditioning we have had. So while diversity comprises facts, inclusion comprises feelings and while diversity targets can be set, inclusion requires a cultural transformation towards an environment where everyone feels like they belong, respected and valued. Remember the old adage "dance like nobody's watching"? That's exactly what we are looking for when we speak of inclusion, an environment where everyone feels like they can dance like nobody's watching.

Now, what about the E that we find between D and I? E stands for equity.

Equity recognises the existence of biases in society and in our workplaces that favour some groups and not others, and makes efforts to compensate for those biases by providing tools, opportunities and support to employees from under-represented, marginalised and discriminated groups. Equity is sometimes confused with a word that sounds rather similar - equality. *Equality* has to do with fairness and focuses on providing everyone with the same tools, opportunities and support, and does not take into account biases and differences in life experiences. What about justice? *Justice* reflects a world free from biases where everyone would have fair and equal experiences, and therefore equal access to tools, opportunities and support. We do not live in a *just* world. Not yet, at least.

ALLYSHIP IN A NUTSHELL

"Please help others rise. Greatness comes not from a position, but from helping build the future. We have an obligation to pull others up."
INDRA NOOYI, former chairperson and CEO of PepsiCo.

Think about the times in your life when you have experienced success - however you choose to define success for yourself. As you reflect on those moments and the journey to get there, were there people who supported you when you could have felt alone? Were there people who nudged you to explore new opportunities that you had not considered before? Perhaps there was someone who recommended you for a new role or promotion at work?

These beautiful experiences of human interaction are moments of allyship.

The term allyship stems from the word ally, and refers to the state of being an ally. As a verb, allyship means *to unite or form a connection or relation between,* and as a noun, it means *a person or group that provides assistance and support in an ongoing effort, activity, or struggle.*[2] Though the word first appeared in English-language sources as far back as the 1840s, its use within the DEI realm can be dated to the 1970s, and was likely derived from the concept of heterosexual support during the LGBT rights movement happening at the time.

Though the word made its way into the Oxford English Dictionary in 2021 and was later named "Word of the Year", the rise in its current usage was in response to the murder of George Floyd in the US and the global racial justice protests which followed. While the term is relatively well known in the US, its awareness and usage is still somewhat limited in other parts of the world, though that is quickly changing. Over the past few years of working as a DEI expert with numerous organisations in various parts of the world, I have found that allyship is often seen as an "American term" and DEI an "American issue". This is far from true. Biases and discrimination exist everywhere, which makes DEI a global issue that needs local solutions to get maximum buy-in from employees in different parts of the world.[3] When it comes to the word *allyship*, finding a one-to-one translation into other languages can be challenging, simply because the words 'ally' and 'allyship' may not exist in other languages. I was recently in a discussion with a client who wanted to translate the word 'allyship' into Danish, and found that it required a full - and fairly long - sentence to capture the meaning. Being conscious and intentional about translating or explaining the term 'allyship' is crucial to increased global awareness and comfort with it. While the word itself may not translate well, what it entails, why it is needed and how it is experienced all resonate deeply across languages and cultures. Why? Because ultimately allyship is all about human interactions and individuals supporting others.

Within the context of DEI, an ally refers to *"a person who is not a member of a marginalised or mistreated group but who expresses or gives support to that group"* [4] and allyship describes the *"extent to which an ally cultivates relationships with others who look different, think different, and/or have different backgrounds and life experiences from them with the conscious intention of nurturing inclusion"*. In this book, allyship is defined as:

> *Allyship (verb)*
>
> A lifelong process of building and nurturing supportive relationships with under-represented, marginalised or discriminated individuals or groups with the aim of advancing inclusion.

What allyship is and isn't

According to a report by Bentley University, allyship is the key to creating inclusive workplaces.[5] The report found that employees of organizations that foster strong allyship are 50% less likely to leave, 56% more likely to improve their performance, 75% less likely to take a sick day, and up to 167% more likely to recommend their organizations as great places to work.[6] Advocates of the concept of allyship see it is as a means to address discrimination and bias in society and workplaces workplaces, and in doing so nurture inclusion. Allyship is often described as an ongoing, consistent and lifelong process.

On the other hand, critics of allyship suggest that it is an ideological, performative, and insincere term, one that actually does more harm than good for the under-represented, marginalised or discriminated.[7] Throughout this book, I will address this criticism by clearly defining what allyship is - and what it is not - as well as providing a guide to allyship to ensure that it is realistic, authentic and sincere.

What allyship is:
- Allyship is a verb, meaning that one has to demonstrate certain behaviours to be considered to be an ally by members of under-represented, marginalised or discriminated groups.
- Allyship is purpose driven; the purpose being to make workplaces and society more inclusive.

- Allyship is authentic.
- Allyship is sincere.
- Allyship is something that is "felt" by others.
- Allyship is about supporting others in a way that is comfortable for them.
- Allyship consists of frequent and consistent behaviours.

What allyship is not:
- Allyship is not performative or to be seen as something to showcase to others.
- Allyship is not about fixing others and "making" the under-represented, marginalised or discriminated conform to dominant norms.
- Allyship is not only about the behaviours performed by the ally but also the impact those behaviours have on others; whether they make others feel included or not.
- Allyship is not about taking away the voice of others, but amplifying their voice.
- Allyship is not made up of isolated behavioural episodes.

Stages of allyship

Think of allyship as a spectrum, made up of a range of behaviours, from denial - not engaging in allyship behaviours - to active - engaging in frequent and consistent behaviours. In between those extremes are a range of passive behaviours. Allyship is a journey we are on; a process of constant progress towards becoming a better, more active ally. The good news is that no matter where you are on this journey, practising the behaviours laid out in this book frequently and consistently will ensure that you move towards active allyship. Becoming an active ally or becoming an even better active ally is a lifelong process. It is about progress rather than perfection.

Stages of Allyship

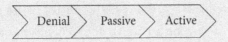

Denial: Someone in the denial stage does not see the need for diversity and does not believe that discrimination is an issue that needs to be addressed. At this stage of allyship, this person prefers to stay in their comfort zone, interacting with those who look and think in similar ways to them, or with whom they share life experiences and backgrounds. Such a person is usually uncomfortable around those who are different from themselves, and resistant to being an ally.

Passive: Someone in the passive stage understands the need for (and benefits of) diversity, and acknowledges the lack of inclusion is a problem to be addressed. At this stage of allyship, this person is in environments where they interact with people who look and think differently from themselves and can identify biases around them, but they do not make any concrete efforts to nurture an inclusive environment primarily because they do not know how to be an ally.

Active: Someone in the active stage keeps themselves well-informed about the latest happenings in the areas of diversity, equity and inclusion, believes that being inclusive is the right thing to do, and is certain of the value that diversity brings. At this stage of allyship, this person is very aware of their own biases; and makes concrete, frequent and consistent efforts to nurture an inclusive environment.

Active allyship

While there will be a certain percentage of people in our organisations who are in the denial stage, the vast majority of us are passive. We simply don't know *how* to be an active ally. When we don't know how to do or be something, we often do nothing. Saying "I'm not racist," (or sexist, ageist or ableist) is not enough. At the same time, many of us are fearful of doing or saying the wrong thing; fearful of confrontation on issues we may not know enough about. However, in that passivity and by doing nothing, we become bystanders and co-conspirators, even if that is not our intention. Our inaction allows discrimination and biases to exist and even thrive.

So, what does it mean to be an *active ally*?

An *active ally* is...

- Acutely aware of their own identity and how their identity intersects with the identities of others.
- One who has a deep understanding of the issues surrounding DEI, which include an understanding of the biases and discrimination across various dimensions of diversity, what challenges individuals from under-represented, marginalised and discriminated groups face, and why it is important to address these.
- One who has the right attitude towards making workplaces more inclusive for all, while promoting and aspiring to advance inclusion through frequent, consistent, intentional, positive and conscious efforts that benefit people as a whole.
- An ally across intersectional dimensions of diversity, not just an ally for some and not others.
- Someone who is brave enough to stand up and openly support under-represented, marginalised or discriminated individuals or groups.

An active ally constantly asks: who is missing from the table? Who isn't in the room who should be there because they bring a perspective and experience that adds value? An active ally understands their responsibility to make workplaces inclusive for all. Does it seem daunting? It is. Yet in order to achieve inclusion, it is exactly what we must do. The aim of this book is to give us the tools and confidence to show up every day: to be an active ally in all workplace situations.

To be effective, active allyship should take place at four levels - individual, interpersonal, team and organisational. The seven behaviours in this book collectively address all four levels. Being an active ally begins with ourselves, as individuals. This self-work is crucial and is the foundation for active allyship at the other three levels. At the interpersonal level active allyship refers to efforts in one-to-one interactions. At the team level, active allyship refers to allyship within team interactions, with teams consisting of three or more members. Finally, at the organisational level, active allyship involves addressing more systemic issues that impact larger groups of people in the organisation.

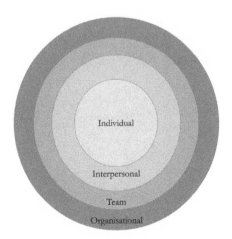

Levels of active allyship

So, how can one become an active ally?

The *Allyship Model* below is based on the Knowledge-Attitude-Behaviour (KAB)[8] approach. In order for us to become active allies, we need to:

- Develop our understanding of the issues at hand (Knowledge).
- Reflect on our biases and the ways in which we engage with others (Attitude).
- Act in ways that build and nurture supportive relationships with others who are under-represented, marginalised or discriminated (Behaviour).

The seven behaviours presented in this book address all three components, many simultaneously.

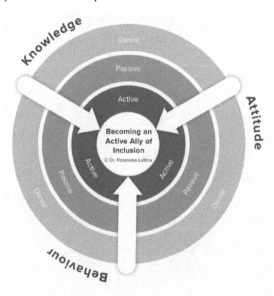

Allyship Model

Inclusive leadership through active allyship

Inclusive leadership is one of the newer leadership styles to join the many other leadership styles required in today's organisations - transformational, charismatic, servant, situational and humane to name a few. The world today is characterised by four major global mega-trends that are reshaping the environment and in turn influencing the priorities of businesses - diversity of markets, diversity of customers, diversity of ideas and diversity of talent.[9] In such a context, the need for inclusive leadership is key. Yet, according to Korn Ferry, only 5% of leaders globally are inclusive.[10]

Inclusive leadership is for everyone in today's workplaces, regardless of whether you have just started your career or if you are a C-suite leader. Don't be put off by the word 'leadership' in the term 'inclusive leadership'. You do not have to be a formal leader with reporting lines. As long as you have a *sphere of influence,* you are indeed a leader with the ability to be a role model for others and to influence them to engage in inclusive behaviours.

In her book *How to Be an Inclusive Leader: Your Role in Creating Cultures of Belonging Where Everyone Can Thrive,*[11] Jennifer Brown, shares that inclusive leaders "can create a culture of belongingness where everyone can thrive in countless ways". In the book *Inclusive Leadership: The Definitive Guide to Developing and Executing an Impactful Diversity and Inclusion Strategy: - Locally and Globally,* authors Charlotte Sweeney and Fleur Bothwick write: "Equality is being invited into the room. Diversity is getting a seat at the table. Inclusion is sharing your views and being heard. An inclusive leader enables all of this to happen."[12]

Inclusive leader

An inclusive leader is one who plays an active part in developing a culture where all individuals are treated fairly and respectfully, have equal access to opportunity and resources, and feel valued, appreciated and a sense of belonging.

According to Deloitte, highly inclusive leaders demonstrate six signature traits "which represent a powerful capability highly adapted to diversity. Inclusive leadership is essential to fostering an environment of empowered well-being, where people are given the support and flexibility they need to be energised, confident, and aware."[13]

These six traits are:[14]

- Commitment
- Courage
- Cognizance of bias
- Curiosity
- Cultural intelligence
- Collaboration

Research by Korn Ferry on leadership assessment data collected from 3 million leaders led to the development of the profile of an inclusive leader consisting of a set of traits and competencies. Their research revealed that an inclusive leader has traits of:[15]

- Authenticity
- Emotional resilience
- Self-assurance
- Flexibility
- Inquisitiveness

An inclusive leader is also someone who demonstrates the following competencies:[16]

- Builds interpersonal trust
- Integrates diverse perspectives
- Optimises talent
- Applies an adaptive mindset
- Achieves transformation

While these models of inclusive leadership are extremely helpful in trying to make sense of what inclusive leadership entails, let us step back and peel away the layers. At the very core of these traits and competencies lie two fundamental ingredients that inclusive leadership depends on:

- The extent to which the leader values diversity, and
- The extent to which the leader is an active ally.

Over many years of working with hundreds of individuals with spheres of influence to potentially be inclusive leaders, I have observed that these two core dimensions of interest play a significant role in determining whether someone is an inclusive leader or not. Even when individuals have the relevant traits and display certain competencies, whether they are an inclusive leader depends on these two dimensions.

For leaders to stop simply acting in the Diversity-Inclusion theatre production and actually walk the talk, they need to truly value diversity and be active allies.

Dimension 1: Valuing diversity

Valuing diversity is not about political correctness, appearing 'woke' or trying to impress. I believe that there should not be a need to justify one's commitment to diversity. It is the right thing to do. Inequality and biases have no place in any workplace. At the same time, it is important for inclusive leaders to recognise, understand and believe in the value of diversity - not to prove or showcase their commitment - but to be one hundred percent convinced themselves. Without this, there will always be an element of resistance or hesitation to be truly inclusive.

> *Valuing diversity*
>
> Valuing diversity is recognising that diversity has the power to make your organisation and team even more effective, more successful, and more profitable. Diversity provides your company access to a greater range of talent and can provide insights into the motivation of your customer or client base.

So where does the value of diversity lie? At the organisational level, 87% of the most admired companies see a positive impact of diversity and inclusion on their business performance.[17] Organisations in the top quartile of gender diversity performed 25% better on profitability if they had gender diverse executive teams, and were 36% more likely to achieve above-average profitability if there is ethnic or cultural diversity among executives.[18] A Credit Suisse study in 2016 found that LGBT-led companies had outperformed the other index companies by 3% annually since 2010,[19] and a 2018 study by Accenture found that businesses that actively seek to employ people with disabilities had revenues that were 28% higher, their net income was two times more, and profit margins were 30% higher than those that do not.[20] Diverse and inclusive organisations are 70% more likely to capture new markets.[21] Gender-diverse boards also tend to adopt more progressive organisational management practices, such as work-life support programs, and to increase employee satisfaction.[22] Those organisations with gender diverse boards have fewer financial reporting mistakes,[23] controversial business practices such as fraud and earnings manipulation,[24] and fewer operations-related lawsuits.[25] Women board directors are also more likely than men to identify social issues like human rights, climate change, and income inequality as critical to corporate strategy.[26]

At the team level, the value of diversity lies in the richness of creative thoughts and the breadth of insights, approaches and perspectives that come from having talent with different backgrounds and experiences. While innovation is limited in homogeneous teams where people see, think and do things in similar ways to each other, innovation flourishes when there are differences.[27] Colleagues who are different from us see things we don't see. Colleagues who are different from us approach things in different ways. Colleagues who are different from us do things differently. It is through these differences that new outcomes - ideas, methods or products - are generated. This is where the magic of diversity lies. Data shows that companies with an inclusive culture and accompanying DEI policies are shown to have a 59.1% increase in creativity, innovation, and openness,[28] with diverse and inclusive teams making better decisions 87% of the time.[29] Diverse and inclusive teams are 76% more likely to see ideas become productized.[30] There is even a direct line between this innovation and profitability: A 2017 BCG report showed that companies with diverse, innovative management teams earned more as a result of that innovation.[31]

For the individual employee, organisations with inclusive work cultures have reduced incidents of interpersonal aggression and discrimination, with women experiencing less discrimination and episodes of sexual harassment.[32] What is really interesting is that just a 10% increase in perceptions of inclusion reduces absenteeism, adding nearly one day a year in work attendance per employee.[33] A 2016 report by the European commission highlights that LGBT-supportive policies are "good for people, good for business" and draws on studies that show that having LGBT-supportive policies reduces incidences of discrimination, thereby improving psychological health and increasing job satisfaction, while also improving relationships between LGBT employees and their colleagues.[34] The US Department of Labour[35] found that employers who embraced disability saw a 90% increase in employee retention.[36] In fact, companies across various industries in India have seen that employing people with disabilities makes sound business sense given the low attrition rates, high productivity, loyalty, and low absenteeism.[37] Similarly, research suggests that neurodiverse employees are 90% to 140% more productive than their neurotypical colleagues because of their increased ability to focus on certain tasks and their ability to concentrate for an extended period of time.[38]

While there is plenty of evidence that supports diversity being good for business, an inclusive leader needs to deeply believe in the intrinsic value of diversity - beyond bottom lines - and be able to convince those who are sceptical through evidence and conviction.

Dimension 2: Active allyship

Valuing diversity is not enough. Inclusive leaders need to walk the talk. It is not enough to simply create and implement a DEI strategy, to make public statements of support or to set, measure and monitor targets. As we have established, it is the *culture of inclusion* that is crucial to harnessing the value of diversity. To harness that value, inclusive leaders must be active allies working to nurture inclusive cultures in their workplaces. Inclusive leaders can do this through the following seven behaviours that we will look at in this book:

- *Deep curiosity* to question the status quo and gain a deeper understanding of the issues surrounding DEI.
- *Honest introspection* to deeply understand bias.
- *Humble acknowledgement* that the world is experienced differently by everyone depending on one's privilege.
- *Empathetic engagement* when addressing biases that we experience or witness.
- *Authentic conversations* that are honest and open in an environment of psychologically safety.
- *Vulnerable interactions* to check biases.
- *Courageous responsibilities* to be inclusive in communication, to lift others and to challenge biases.

Putting these two dimensions of interest together - the value placed on diversity and the extent of active allyship - provides us with a typology of four DEI leadership styles.

- **Disengaged leader:** Someone who values homogeneity or limited dimensions of diversity that they are comfortable with, such as supporting those that have the same gender identity or ethnicity, and who displays few, if any, active allyship behaviours. This leader is usually in the denial stage of allyship. They may exhibit some limited forms of passive allyship within the dimensions of diversity they are comfortable with.

- **Tribal leader:** Someone who values homogeneity or limited dimensions of diversity that they are comfortable with, such as supporting those that have the same gender identity or ethnicity, and displays active allyship to those within the tribe but not outside it.

- **Pluralistic leader:** Someone who values diversity and lets diverse groups exist as separate entities rather than as a cohesive team or organisation, and who displays few, if any, active allyship behaviours. This leader is usually in the passive stage of allyship, recognising the need for diversity but not being able or willing to be an active player in nurturing inclusion. Such a leader may, for example, be happy for Pride events to take place, but not attend those events or engage actively throughout the year to make the workplace inclusive for their LGBTQIA+ colleagues.

- **Inclusive leader:** Someone who values and believes in diversity, and who is an active ally across intersectional identities, bringing them together as an inclusive team or organisation to harness the value of diversity for the organisation, team and the individuals themselves. There are incredible leaders who do this, but it is something we should all aspire to.

Where do you think you lie? Do you recognise these DEI leadership styles in others?

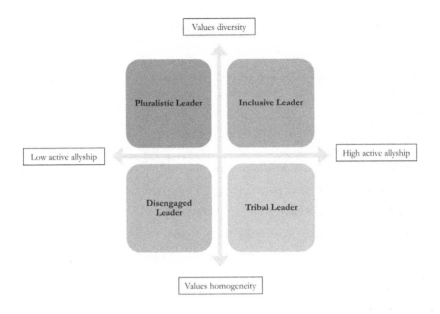

DEI leadership styles

Now that you have a good grasp of what allyship, active allyship and inclusive leadership are, we are ready to delve into the seven behaviours of active allyship. These seven behaviours include all the tools you need to be an active ally as an individual, in your interactions with others, as a team member and as an employee of an organisation. The journey to becoming an active ally won't be easy, and at times it will be frustrating and require us to be vulnerable, but the reward - diverse and inclusive workplaces for all - and the benefits that come with truly inclusive workspaces - should act as a motivation for us to become active allies.

Every journey starts with a first step. On your journey to being an active ally, the first step is to identify what stage of active allyship you are currently at. On the next page you will find a checklist to help you determine where you are now. It is only when we know the starting point that we will know where to begin this journey of active allyship.

What stage of allyship am I at?

To use the *Allyship Model*, the most important step is to first identify your current stage of allyship: Denial, Passive or Active. It is important to note that where we are along this journey towards active allyship can vary across the three components of Knowledge-Attitude-Behaviour. We may have the knowledge and attitude to be an active ally, but our behaviour may be more passive in nature. Or we may have the knowledge about being an active ally but need to develop our beliefs and attitude to help us make our behaviours more active.

Spend some time reading the descriptions for each stage below and mark where you think you are at present for each of the following components - Knowledge, Attitude and Behaviour. Be honest with yourself. Only when we know and recognise where we are, can we decide where we want to go.

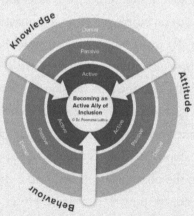

Knowledge

Active:
- ☐ I have a deep understanding of DEI.
- ☐ I have a good command of DEI vocabulary and feel comfortable to use it.
- ☐ I keep myself well-informed of the latest developments in the area of DEI, locally and globally, through books, articles and reports.
- ☐ I organise and/or participate in communities of practise to share what I know and learn.

Passive:
- ☐ I have a basic understanding of DEI.
- ☐ I have basic command of DEI vocabulary but hesitate to use it.
- ☐ I understand and appreciate the need for DEI.
- ☐ I understand the limitations of homogeneity.

Denial:
- ☐ I do not understand the need for DEI and see no necessity to make an effort to understand more about DEI.
- ☐ I am not familiar with DEI vocabulary.
- ☐ I appreciate the benefits of homogeneity and working with people similar to me, and make efforts to find evidence to support this.
- ☐ I recognise the benefits of conforming to the accepted norms defined by the majority.

Attitude

Active:
- ☐ I believe in the value of diversity and that being inclusive is the right thing to do.
- ☐ I believe in the benefits of effective unconscious bias training.
- ☐ I have a positive mindset towards being aware of my own biases and privileges.
- ☐ I believe in the power of having a set of colleagues with whom I can check my biases with.

Passive:
- ☐ I believe that DEI are needed.
- ☐ I feel comfortable with bias training.
- ☐ I view discrimination as an issue that needs to be addressed.
- ☐ I keep an open mind to being aware of my own biases and privileges.

Denial:
- ☐ I believe that DEI do not concern me.
- ☐ I do not believe that discrimination is an issue that needs attention.
- ☐ I believe I am unbiased.
- ☐ I do not believe in the need for bias training.

Behaviour

Active:

- ☐ I actively speak about the benefits of DEI.
- ☐ I call out biases and microaggressions using respectful questioning.
- ☐ I engage frequently in open and honest dialogues about DEI with those around me.
- ☐ I make sincere efforts to make decisions that support diversity and foster inclusion.
- ☐ I make conscious efforts to correct systemic biases in systems, policies and practices.
- ☐ I actively include, sponsor and mentor those from minority groups.
- ☐ I set up and/or participate in Employee Resource Groups for minority groups.
- ☐ I put pressure on managers and leaders to take concrete actions.

Passive:

- ☐ I can identify biases and microaggressions but feel uncomfortable calling them out.
- ☐ I am comfortable interacting with others who look and think differently than me.
- ☐ I seek opportunities to be amongst diverse groups of people.
- ☐ I am comfortable being a part of uncomfortable discussions on discrimination, though I do not actively participate in them.
- ☐ I recognise systemic bias in systems, processes and practices.
- ☐ My way of supporting minority groups and DEI initiatives involves not opposing it.
- ☐ I notice when those from minority groups feel excluded, though I am not sure what to do about it.
- ☐ I celebrate others who are being an active ally.

Denial:

☐ I do not notice biases and microaggressions, and am unable to identify them.

☐ I feel uncomfortable when discussing discrimination and bias.

☐ I interact with others who look and think like I do.

☐ I feel unsure of what to say and do when there are people who are different from me.

☐ I prefer being in situations that are familiar to me.

☐ I actively avoid being amongst diverse groups of people.

☐ I get uncomfortable when there are minority groups around me.

☐ I am uncomfortable with DEI initiatives and do not think they are necessary

THE 7 ACTIVE ALLYSHIP BEHAVIOURS

1
DEEP
CURIOSITY

"Fear is incomplete knowledge"

AGATHA CHRISTIE,
19ᵗʰ century British author

Being an active ally begins with ourselves - with a *deep curiosity*; a curiosity to both question the status quo and to gain a deeper understanding of the issues surrounding DEI.

Let's begin with cookie cutters. What on earth do cookie cutters have to do with DEI? Bear with me a moment.

Have you ever baked or bought or even eaten cookies? What have you noticed about the shape of those cookies? Usually within a batch or tray of cookies, each cookie looks the same. To achieve this level of sameness, we are likely to use a cookie cutter in the shape of a star, heart, a gingerbread person...you get the picture. By using a cookie cutter, we ensure that all the cookies are exactly the same shape and size - a homogenous tray of cookies. All delicious but exactly the same.

We find cookie cutters not just in our kitchens - where they belong - but in our workplaces as well.

Think of the people who are considered to be successful in your organisation. Do they have more in common with each other than differences? Do they have the same skin colour, age, gender, or sexual orientation? Have they had similar educational and socio-economic backgrounds? Do they have similar leadership qualities? Are they extroverted? Do they communicate well and are they able to think on their feet? Are they all able-bodied and conform to what is accepted as neurotypical? Do they outsource childcare and household responsibilities to others? As you think about the answers to these questions, see if an image begins to form. What makes up the "cookie cutter" of a successful person in your organisation? What does that mean for those who do not "fit" this cookie cutter? Are the same opportunities available to them? Do they experience the workplace in the same way as those who "fit" the cookie cutter?

Our workplaces seem to celebrate talent that conforms to a certain cookie cutter - or prototype - of an ideal employee. Very often, the prototype is a White, heterosexual, able-bodied male. This cookie-cutter approach to hiring and promoting talent has had a tremendous impact on many aspects of organisational life. It influences who we hire to join the team or lead the company, the hours we work, when meetings are scheduled, and crucially, workplace culture. We have been socially conditioned to accept these without question; until now that is.

The reality is that we often hire and promote people who are similar to ourselves or others in the team. We assume that they are more likely to "fit in", perform well on the job and work well with us and our colleagues. By default, anyone with a different set of experiences and skills, different ways of working or different life experiences may not "fit in", and therefore, the assumption is that they won't be as successful at their jobs and within their teams. We rely on this *affinity bias* and conclude that a particular person will be better suited for a job, and we often use the excuse that someone who is different from others in that role is "not a good fit". We should be asking ourselves what are we expecting the candidate to fit into?

Hiring for "fit" has no place in an organisation seeking to be diverse and looking to benefit from that diversity. I often challenge the leaders I work with to remove the words "fit" and "normal" from their corporate dictionaries. As difficult as that seems, it is necessary if we are to truly have inclusive organisations for talent from intersectional identities. So the next time you hear "this person was not a good fit", question that decision. Be curious to understand on what basis that decision was made. Was it truly because the person's values did not align with the organisation's? Or perhaps the individual did not meet the needs of the role because they did not "fit" the cookie cutter? In the words of Nigerian author Chimamanda Ngozi Adichie: "If we do something over and over again, it becomes normal. If we see the same thing over and over again, it becomes normal...If we keep seeing only men as heads of corporations, it starts to seem 'natural' that only men should be heads of corporations."[39]

This cookie-cutter phenomenon is pervasive, and expectations to "fit" the cookie cutter are strong. Have you observed that women in senior leadership positions often display many of the same traits and behaviours as their male counterparts? This is not accidental. Women in leadership roles feel pressured to modify the way they act, lead, behave and even dress or speak to be able to climb the corporate ladder. On a panel with senior leaders in a large pharmaceutical company, a female leader mentioned that when she became part of the executive team she was told "but you're one of us". While it was probably meant as a compliment, it did not sit well with her. Given that the rest of the team was made up of men, she took time to reflect on how much she has changed herself to "fit in". Her story is far from unique.

I once had a female C-suite leader tell me that "The only difference between me and my male peers is that I have breasts and a vagina. I behave like them; I think like them. I went to the same universities, followed similar career pathways to the top, do not have childcare responsibilities and yes, I also drink beer like them. I even wear only pantsuits, never a dress or skirt! I have learnt that this is what it takes to get to the top." The handful of women who have reached the echelons of the corporate hierarchy often feel fearful of losing their position and opportunities if they try to do things in their own way. Instead, they put in a tremendous effort to conform to the dominant norms because that is what gets rewarded in our workplaces. It is difficult to find evidence of acceptance, or even tolerance, for deviation from the prescribed cookie cutter.

Let me also ask you this: Who do you think is considered to be an ideal employee? Is it someone who is deeply committed? By committed, you may think of someone who sacrifices personal priorities and family responsibilities to further one's career. This likely involves working long hours in the office, late nights and weekends or attending to work demands as and when the need arises, even dropping personal commitments to make that happen. This ideal is in direct conflict with our ideas of ideal parenthood, and motherhood more specifically. Many working mothers feel pressured to leave their motherhood behind when they enter the workplace in order to be seen by others as professional and an equal contributor. Imagine how many times a woman of childbearing age - regardless of whether she actually wants children or not - is overlooked as a potential candidate for a role, regardless of how amazing her CV is, how well she interviewed, or how much value she could add to the team. The assumption is that she would not "fit" the cookie cutter: the mould of the committed, successful employee.

Being in the office - and seen to be visibly doing work - has long been seen as part of what makes up the cookie cutter of a successful employee. Through the COVID-19 pandemic that began towards the end of 2019, these expectations and assumptions of work needing to be done in the office have been shaken to the core. Across the world, there was a recognition that there are many jobs (certainly not all) that can actually be done remotely in part, if not all. Yes, we need to interact face-to-face with colleagues to build teamwork but perhaps not every day or for 40 hours a week. While there seems to be a pressure to return to old ways from some leaders (not all), there is also a strong desire from employees to retain that flexibility and move towards hybrid forms of working. Being physically present in the office for long hours - part of that cookie cutter mould - is being challenged.

So while we have leaders like Elon Musk insisting on employees being in the office working a minimum of 40 hours a week,[40] fortunately we are also seeing many other companies like Microsoft, Facebook, Dell, American Express[41] and Salesforce[42] embracing flexible working options globally. Why? Because flexible work arrangements can help companies become more diverse and inclusive. Flexibility is really about choice - the choice to manage your calendar and schedule according to your own personal priorities. Choosing where to work, in the office or at home or in a hybrid format, is part of that choice. Having the option of working flexibly expands the talent pool from which companies can hire from. Given the talent shortage we are facing in present times globally, this can only be a boon.

What is extremely interesting is the data. The Great Resignation that occurred during the pandemic saw a disproportionate number of women leave the workforce in parts of the world where the pandemic raged through. With schools closed and children home in remote learning, and given the widespread gender bias in who the primary caregiver of children is, many women were forced to leave their jobs. Flexible work arrangements - alongside good childcare options - are certainly key in getting women back into the workforce. But it is not just women who stand to benefit from flexible work arrangements.

A pulse survey from over 10,000 knowledge workers in the U.S., France, Germany and other countries by Future Forum[43] found that the desire for flexibility remains strongest among under-represented groups. In the U.S., 81% of Hispanic/Latinx workers, 82% of Asian/ Asian American and 79% Black workers prefer a hybrid of remote work arrangements compared to 77% of white workers. What is also interesting is that the rise in remote work has also coincided with higher employee experience scores among Black employees. Black employees are reporting a greater "sense of belonging" at work (up 10%) and a stronger sense of being "fairly treated" at work (up 7%) compared to November 2021.[44]

Under-represented ethnicities often feel the need to leave their cultural background behind and make conscious efforts to "fit-in" with the dominant norms of behaviour. This can take the form of code switching - speaking or acting in a different way to "fit in", straightening one's natural hair to conform to the dominant group's idea of professionalism, or hiding religious symbols to avoid discrimination. A single dad may feel the pressure to leave fatherhood out of the office to be seen as a team player. A gay employee may experience fear, forcing them to hide their sexual orientation. When the talent in our organisations feel compelled to conform to the organisation's cookie cutter to be accepted, it puts a tremendous emotional and mental strain on them. This can lead to resentment and contributes to feelings of not belonging; of not being included.

If our expectation is to get employees from under-represented groups to do things the way it has always been done, are we really embracing the value of diversity? In a business world that is faced with constant disruption and change, being able to innovate is crucial to survival. Innovation requires people who are able to think differently from the way the company and industry has done before. To be able to differentiate themselves from competitors, companies need people who are looking at their product lines and services in novel ways. If innovation is needed, diversity is key. Crayola's Colours of the World[45] crayons, Nike's FlyEase[46] laceless shoes and ANKHGER's MagZip[47] would not have been possible without embracing diversity. Given their different life experiences, those from under-represented, marginalised and discriminated groups see and do things *differently*. That's where the magic of diversity lies. Trying to make those outside the mould fit into the cookie cutter defeats the very purpose of promoting and valuing diversity. We don't want more of the same.

We want the difference. We want different ways of communicating, different ways of managing, different educational and work experiences, different ways of thinking about challenges, different solutions. If we hire employees from under-represented groups and then expect them - and even shape them - to be like everyone else, like the cookie cutter, we have destroyed the very benefits of diversity that we could have gained.

In the words of Alexander Den Heijer, a Dutch inspirational speaker, trainer, and consultant: "When a flower doesn't bloom, you fix the environment in which it grows, not the flower." It's time to stop hiring for "fit". Cookie cutters belong in kitchen drawers, not in our workplaces.

To nurture inclusive workplaces, and encourage hiring and promoting more diversely, we need active allies to step up and question the status quo - question the cookie cutters. The courage to do this requires us to have a deep understanding of the issues at hand. Often when we don't know enough about something, we do not engage in it. Why? Because we might be fearful of getting things wrong, of saying the wrong things, of being misunderstood or misrepresented. So how do we address this fear? In the wise words of the 19th century American poet and philosopher, Ralph Waldo Emerson: "Knowledge is the antidote to fear." In the area of DEI, that means having a curiosity to get deeper into the issues surrounding DEI, beyond being able to regurgitate your company's DEI vision statements and strategy. To be an active ally means having a deep understanding. You can only have a deep understanding when you are deeply curious.

While we may have some understanding about biases related to race, ethnicity, gender, sexual orientation, age and disabilities, there are many other dimensions of diversity that give rise to biases and discrimination that are experienced in the workplace that we have much less of an understanding of. Even with the relatively better-known biases, how many of us truly understand the history, experiences and implications of these biases? Understanding the fuller picture is the key to being better informed and reducing fear.

More recently, there has been increased discussion in business-related publications like *Harvard Business Review* about the need to address workplace biases more broadly; biases based on sexual orientation, physical disabilities, age and most recently, neurodiversity. While gender and ethnicity are the predominant dimensions in organisations' efforts to make their workplaces more diverse and inclusive, other dimensions have not yet received the attention or traction needed. Gender and ethnicity are extremely important, and we need to continue the work in these areas. At the same time, the diversity of human beings is much more than our gender and ethnicity; it includes age, physical abilities, physical appearance, our educational background, skills, ways of working, learning and thinking, our sexual orientation, beliefs and values, socio-economic background and the choices we make about marriage and parenthood. Our *diversity thumbprint* reflects our identity in many of these dimensions, and the intersectionality of these dimensions - where they meet - is where the complexity of biases and discrimination lie. It just so happens that is also where the potential magic and value to organisations and society reside.

In 2021, I published my book *Diversifying Diversity*.[48] My journey with diversifying diversity actually began with a professional experience. I had been teaching for a few years after having completed my PhD and had solid teaching and peer evaluations. I was ready for more, for a new challenge. As it turned out, there was an opportunity to teach a Masters course and I approached my Head of Department at the time and suggested that I would like to be considered for the role. He looked at me and said: "Not until you have a lot more white hair." Here I was - a woman of colour - but gender and race were not the dimensions of diversity upon which I was being discriminated on. It was my age. This started my research and work in getting companies to put more on the diversity table; to be more inclusive to their employees' entire diversity thumbprint.

In *Diversifying Diversity*, I take an in-depth research-based look at the biases in each of the 12 dimensions below that I believe are the most relevant for today's organisations. These dimensions are divided into three categories: *physical and physiological, cognitive* as well as *social and lifestyle*. Gender, sexual orientation, and age, along with physical abilities and appearances, constitute the physical and physiological dimensions of diversity. The cognitive dimension looks at diversity in education, experiences and skills, personality, and ways of working, as well as ways of thinking and learning. Finally, the social and lifestyle category includes the diversity of ethnicity and culture, beliefs and practices, and marital and parenthood choices in addition to socio-economic background. Some of these dimensions are visible, others are invisible. Each person has a diversity thumbprint consisting of some combination of many, if not all, of these 12 dimensions of diversity. This thumbprint consisting of a person's intersectional identities is unique to each one of us.

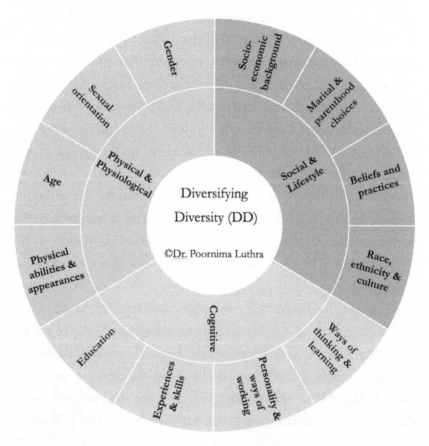

Dimensions of Diversity

These dimensions of diversity - and the many biases arising from them - affect many aspects of organisational life. They play a role in who gets hired and who does not; how employees progress through the organisation; the opportunities they are given; how they are assessed; and how they are rewarded. It may affect how someone dresses for work or their preferred working hours or even what motivates them. These dimensions of diversity can influence how someone prefers to be led or how they lead others, the ways in which they communicate and how they prefer to receive or provide feedback. They can even have an impact on the ways in which the physical space of the workplace is laid out, making provisions for those with physical disabilities, those who are neurodiverse, or those with religious requirements such as the need for prayer rooms.

Most importantly - and often forgotten - are that these dimensions of diversity and their related biases do not exist in isolation; they intersect with each other to form the complex weave of diversity which is unique to each person. For example, I am not just a woman. I am so much more than that - I am a Generation X heterosexual woman who is an ethnically Indian-Singaporean living in Denmark. I lean towards being more introverted than extroverted, follow a plant-based lifestyle and am married with two children. That is my diversity thumbprint - my intersectional identity. To truly embrace diversity and nurture inclusive workplaces, we must recognise this intersectionality. We must acknowledge the interplay between the dimensions of diversity because the experiences of bias and discrimination that result are in turn intensified. While intersectionality makes diversity even more complex to unpack, understand and manage, it is absolutely necessary if we want to nurture inclusive workplaces for all.

To develop this depth of understanding, we need to be curious. We need to build our knowledge base about issues in the area of diversity, equity and inclusion. We need to understand where biases and discrimination come from. We need to listen with curiosity, not simply to respond, but to learn from the experiences of bias and discrimination from those from under-represented, marginalised and discriminated groups. Not knowing the full extent of the biases that exist means that we are unable to address them. This curiosity and thirst to know more can be met through accessing the wealth of resources many of us have access to. In recent years, there has been an explosion of books, articles, and podcasts from credible sources that help us gain this deeper understanding.

As someone working in the DEI field, I am often asked what the various letters of LGBTQIA+ stand for, or why someone chooses to wear a turban, bindi or hijab. The good thing is that we do not need to ask those questions of someone who identifies with these dimensions; the information is available at our fingertips. The responsibility is on us; we need to be curious enough to seek this knowledge out without placing the burden on others to explain their identities or their life choices to us.

One of the easiest and most practical ways in which we can practise deep curiosity is to find out how to pronounce another person's name correctly. What does a name have to do with diversity and inclusion? A lot, actually. How many "different" sounding names do you notice in your team? Are they pronounced fully and accurately? While having employees from a variety of backgrounds is an opportunity to leverage the benefits of a diverse workforce, we need to ensure that our workplaces are creating a sense of belonging where every employee can bring their whole diverse selves to work - including difficult-to-pronounce names - and feel fully accepted.

Research shows that *name discrimination* - biases based on some-one's name - runs deep and has significant implications on employees' experiences of inclusion. Mispronouncing a person's name is so com-monplace that those with "different" sounding names sometimes do not even bother to correct others. While mispronunciation seems to be normalised, don't be mistaken that it doesn't matter. It absolutely does. It makes the person whose name is being mispronounced feel like they are "different" from others with "easier" to pronounce names. A name is so much more than just an identifier. Our names reflect our rich her-itage, ethnicity and culture, background, family, and in all this – our identity. When the mispronunciation happens repeatedly, it can make the person feel disrespected and unvalued.

I have Chinese, Vietnamese and Japanese friends and colleagues with supposedly difficult-to-pronounce names who have informally taken on western names like 'Angela' and 'Peter' just to be able to fit in. I have had friends and colleagues ask if there was a shorter form of my name - Poornima - that would make it easier for them. In fact, I went through high school and college known as "Nima" because I could not bear the sound of friends and teachers mispronouncing my name. More recently, I have noticed that colleagues prefer to refer to me as "P" rather than writing my full name out in an email or other forms of communication, but seem perfectly comfortable with typing out other eight-letter Anglo-Saxon names in the same correspondence. On one such instance, when I addressed it with the person, their response was "I was multitasking and busy, maybe it isn't such a big deal?" Except it is a big deal, because it highlights the difference - that they had time to type out names that they were comfortable with but not mine. Imagine how the act itself and subsequent dismissal of my feelings made me feel; not included for sure.

Pronouncing someone's name correctly is our first chance to be an active ally. The next time you meet someone with what may be an unfamiliar or difficult to pronounce name for you, be curious and ask them for the right pronunciation, and don't worry if you don't get it right the first time. Take a chance and try.

The next step is to become part of DEI communities of practice in your organisation. *Communities of practice* in the workplace bring people together to discuss DEI issues in a psychologically safe environment. These communities can act as a forum for the exchange of ideas or can be action-oriented in their mandate. Engaging in conversations with colleagues, or even with our network outside, can help expand our knowledge base and build our understanding around the issues in the area of bias and DEI.

In most organisations today, these communities of practice exist as Employee Resource Groups (ERGs), bringing together under-represented employees and often their allies to create a safe space for discussion, for sharing concerns and increasing awareness across the organisation of the challenges they face through campaigns, events or workshops. Some argue that these ERGs discriminate against anyone who isn't under-represented.

My answer to that is clear. Until we get to a time when everyone is indeed treated equally with equal opportunities, we need to create platforms and spaces for under-represented, marginalised and discriminated groups to feel a sense of community, a sense of belonging, and a sense of psychological safety - a place where they feel that their experiences are not isolated.

ERGs welcome allies. So become a part of an ERG or two with colleagues with whom you do not share intersectional identities. Be curious. Listen to their conversations and concerns. Do not get defensive. Do not dismiss their experiences as being isolated or untrue. Do not jump to solutions. Just listen with a desire to want to know more. Let this deep curiosity help you question the status quo - the cookie cutter. Active allyship begins with deep curiosity.

Deep curiosity means:
- Questioning and challenging the cookie cutter, the status quo, who is considered to be a good "fit" or what is considered normal.
- Seeking out knowledge from credible sources on biases and discriminatory practices across a range of intersectional dimensions of diversity to increase understanding.
- Learning how to pronounce other people's names.
- Joining Employee Resource Groups (ERGs) or communities of practice.
- Listening without being dismissive or getting defensive.

Diversifying my understanding of diversity

To begin your journey of active allyship, take a look at the dimensions of diversity below and answer the questions that follow to help you identify what you want to be more curious about. Once you know which dimensions of diversity you want to know more about, seek out the knowledge. Be curious.

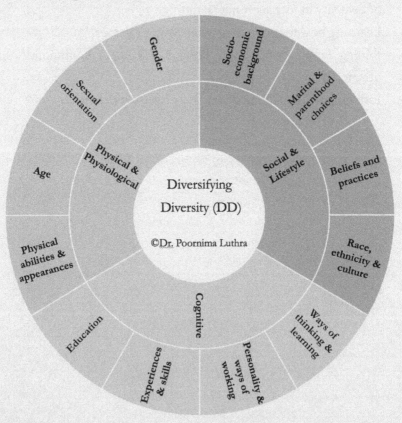

Which dimensions of diversity would you use to describe your identity?

....
....
....
....
....
....

Which dimensions of diversity did you not use to describe your identity?

....
....
....
....
....
....
....

Which dimensions of diversity have the greatest effect on how others perceive you? Explain.

....
....
....
....
....
....

Which dimensions of diversity - and the resulting biases and discrimination - are you most familiar with?

....
....
....
....
....
....
....
....
....

Which dimensions of diversity are you most curious to learn more about? What would you like to do to find out more about these dimensions? Be as specific as you can be. List books or articles to read, podcasts to listen to or other sources of information. You may wish to explore the section 'Recommended Sources' at the end of this book for ideas.

....
....
....
....
....
....
....
....
....

Are there any dimensions of diversity that make you feel uncomfortable? Reflect upon why that may be the case. Could it be related to parenting and educational influences? Could it be due to cultural norms or past experiences?

....
....
....
....
....
....
....
....
....

List the dimensions of diversity that define who is successful in your organisation. Reflect on the dimensions that are missing, and consider the value to the organisation of having someone who identifies with those dimensions.

....
....
....
....
....
....
....
....
....

Emil Novák-Tót (He/Him)

I'm a queer disabled Hungarian immigrant with ADHD, who is also a trans man. I'm also the first one from my family who went to university.

My story here is based on the following intersectional dimensions of diversity: Gender - Sexual orientation - Disabilities - Physical appearances - Neurodiversity - Race, ethnicity and culture - Socio-economic background

Here is my story of bias and discrimination…

It's such a tricky thing, because how do you know you're not getting the same opportunities specifically because of X and Y, right? In a previous job, I watched all my German colleagues being offered permanent positions while me and the one other Eastern European colleague of mine were constantly kept on the exploitative student contract. Then again, I have been denied medical attention on the same basis before: a doctor in the Netherlands refused to give me a tetanus shot because my country "is covered in chicken shit anyway, eh?" I watched my parents be abused and completely overworked as immigrants in Germany. At the same time, I experienced similar abuse and exploitation as an immigrant. Unfortunately, I have post-traumatic stress disorder (PTSD) from that particular time in my life, and the company still owes me 50% of my salary that I'll probably never see because there was no contract to protect me. (Though these experiences are an important part of my journey, I genuinely don't presume to compare the xenophobia my family has experienced to the racism immigrants and other people of colour experience in Europe).

I've been spat at on the street for being queer, and harassed for being in public with my partner, both in the Netherlands and in Denmark. At a former workplace, I was asked by my manager to be the queer face for their diversity campaign on social media. In the same week, I listened to that same manager refer to others like me who she would see on the NYC subway as "shameless freaks, men dressed like women and vice versa". What a truly wild place that company was! The irony was lost on everyone else, and I sat there with my face burning at the lunch table.

I've also faced humiliation at that same workplace explicitly because of my ADHD. I'm also chronically ill and physically disabled - I walk with a crutch on the worst of days while on better days, I only look like I'm okay. Not once have I been warned or asked about potential accessibility issues or questions to prepare for upcoming company events. What that means for me is that often I will spend my weekends in bed where nobody can see me, fearful of being seen as an underperformer. I've heard it all before.

I think what people don't really get is that a lot of us marginalised folks have faced so many traumatising experiences (with many others experiencing so much more discrimination than me) at workplaces that we carry that baggage with us, unable to shake it off. Voicing my needs isn't that easy when my needs have been branded as incompetent, underperforming and lacking motivation so many times before. My queerness is seen as eccentric and shoving my lifestyle in other people's faces. It's not enough to passively be open to people bringing their whole self to work. Unless I'm explicitly and enthusiastically invited to do so, I won't know it's safe. And even so, it'll take time and I will be anxious about it.

Here is how you can be an active ally to someone like me...

If you get my pronouns wrong, just correcting yourself and moving on is enough, and in fact the best way forward. Providing a big apology and explaining why it's so hard to get it right is all about your feelings. I also don't always have the emotional bandwidth to correct someone. So if you hear someone use the wrong pronouns, correcting them - even if I am not in the room - is such a wonderful way to be supportive.

It's okay to ask about my gender or my sexuality. There is no need to dance around topics or assume things; nothing good has ever come out of that. As long as you respect me saying no to answering some questions, you can just ask and let me decide if I want to share.

Not assuming my limits for me is always appreciated. It's about autonomy. I may be disabled, but I'm an adult. If I said no to an offer of help, please respect it. When you see me balancing things and my crutch, don't take things out of my hand without asking.

Not making jokes about my ADHD goes a long way, too. This one might seem obvious, but surprisingly I don't think it is to many people. On that same note, not misusing terms like ADHD, OCD, bipolar, narcissist to describe personality traits like forgetfulness, liking to organise things, having mood swings and being a jerk, respectively, will help halt the stigmatisation of such conditions.

If you are ready to do more, educate yourself and support the fight against the systemic issues that affect the people you may or may not know, and advocate for their rights. My country is passing one trans- and queerphobic legislation after the other. Disabled people face significant financial and social inequity everywhere, and the more intersections of marginalizations, the worse it gets. Educate others, speak up when you see harassment or injustice, challenge discrimination and prejudice in private and professional circles. Hold your company leaders accountable about accommodation and emergency evacuation policies (remember elevators can't be used when there's a fire), push for accessibility policies, initiate conversations about hybrid workplaces etc. I have to believe that we can make the world a more liveable place for everyone, together.

Chisom Udeze (She/Her)

I am a Black cis-gendered heterosexual woman of African heritage, Nigerian, to be more precise. My formative years were in the U.S. and as such, a part of my identity has been significantly influenced by American culture. I have also spent most of the past 13 years in Europe, living, learning, working and evolving in countries like the Netherlands and the United Kingdom. In early 2020, I became a Norwegian citizen, and continue to acquire aspects of Norwegian culture in my cultural repertoire. So, I tend to say that I identify primarily as Nigerian, but also American and most recently, a naturalised Norwegian citizen.

I am a daughter, sister, aunty, mother, wife and friend. I live with an invisible disability.

Professionally, I am an Economist and, in this regard, I work with organizations across the world. I am also an entrepreneur, a founder of three thriving companies, and an employer in Norway. I am a DEIB (diversity-equity-inclusion-belonging) strategist and data enthusiast. I endeavour to use an equity and intersectional lens in all I do. I am an avid learner and un-learner. I actively seek out new information on various topics.

My story here is based on the following intersectional dimensions of diversity: Gender - Sexual orientation - Age - Disabilities - Physical appearances - Educational background - Experiences and skills - Personality - Neurodiversity - Race, ethnicity and culture - Beliefs and practices - Marital and parenthood choices - Socio-economic background

Here is my story of bias and discrimination...

I face discrimination on the basis of my gender, race and various intersectionalities. At present, I do not particularly feel up for rehashing them in detail. I can nonetheless say that I am often not expected. I walk into many professional settings - often for the first time - where people are depending on my decision to move ahead and before they realize who I am, they might think I am the "help". It has been an interesting experience watching people scramble to talk themselves out of their sometimes unconscious and conscious biases. I am also well aware that many, including myself, continue to face discrimination on a basis of what makes us human - such as gender identity, LGBTQIA+ status, race, age, disability and other identifiers. There is much work yet to be done.

Here is how you can be an active ally to someone like me...

I think that the word allyship has become another buzzword. So, one might think it's enough to use a hashtag or show up to a rally. And in many ways, doing things like these are a start. Nonetheless, I am often interested in what happens afterwards and on an ongoing basis. Allyship is an active state of being, learning and unlearning. As Dr. Yaba Blay puts it (and I paraphrase) switching the word allyship to accomplice might give us a better understanding of what it actually takes to be an ally. This analogy (an ally as an accomplice) is for nuance purposes only. I neither condone nor encourage participation in criminal activity.

For me, the best way to be an ally is to show up, even when one has something to lose. Showing up can mean different things in different contexts. Sometimes, something as simple and thoughtful as a message is always appreciated. Given that allyship is contextual, I believe it is important to "do the work". Doing the work means taking responsibility for self-education on the relevant historical, socio-economic, political and environmental backdrop, and not relying on me to "teach" or offer resources. Take the time to conduct research, read relevant and nuanced books and articles, lean into the discomfort, introspect, learn and then act.

Being an ally means that to some degree, you understand your privilege and power, and endeavour to translate them into action in spaces where you have the ability to act. Privilege is fluid and evolving. Resultantly, anyone of us can be an ally, depending on the context. Acknowledging that we have privilege is not a zero-sum game or an invitation to engage in the "Oppression Olympics". You can have privilege in one room and lack it in another room. Knowing where we have privilege, based on our identities, might help us become better allies to people around us.

Allyship requires humility, creating and holding space for others, and decentring ourselves in the discourse. Ultimately, due to the contextual and personal nature of allyship, when in doubt, it is best to never make an assumption, you can always ask, rather than assume. For example, what works for your neurodiverse or non-binary friend, might not work for another neurodiverse or non-binary person.

Fahad Saeed (He/Him)

16 years ago, I co-founded Sabaah, an organization for ethnic minority LGBT+ persons, which has given me a platform to work professionally with D&I. Today, I work with Danish and International companies and organizations facilitating training sessions, workshops and conversations in the intersectional spectrum of D&I (DEIA). In Denmark, I am a well-known public speaker and sit on the boards of prestigious organizations such as KVINFO and Mino Denmark.

My story here is based on the following intersectional dimensions of diversity: Gender - Sexual orientation - Age - Disabilities - Physical appearances - Educational background - Experiences and skills - Neurodiversity - Race, ethnicity and culture - Beliefs and practices - Marital and parenthood choices - Socio-economic background

Here is my story of bias and discrimination…

I have a masters degree in communication and Danish, and have years of experience as a public speaker. My large network is made up of academics, activists and political stakeholders. My life partner is a tall white cis-gendered Danish citizen.

As odd as this may sound, these factors shield me from direct discrimination as they provide me with spaces with less direct discrimination. But my skin is brown; my parents are Pakistani. I am a gay man who grew up in a Muslim lower middle class home, where my parents struggled to make ends meet, raising four children and getting us through school and university.

There are situations where I am no more than these factors - brown skin, foreign passport holder and Muslim - at border controls, interactions with the police in restaurants and even in some work settings.

Migration is an integral part of my identity as my parents migrated not just once, but three times in their lives. From India to Pakistan, in pre-partition times. Then onto the UK where they created a life and started a family before deciding on settling down in Denmark which is where I grew up. As an adult, I am able to see not only my upbringing, but also my parents and my family's story, through this lens of a trans-generational legacy with everything that it entails - good, bad, traumatic and healing.

As a young adult, I struggled to make - what I later could describe as my intersectional identity - fit the normative narrative of fitting in; desiring to be more middle class, more Danish, perhaps even more white or light skinned, and definitely more straight and cis-gendered.

On top of that, I struggled with navigating in my own community and family life. I cannot begin to unravel that part of my life, but I hope you allow me to leave it described as complicated, at many times painful but also beautiful, rich and something that I would never want to be without.

This is my story. It is connected to the stories of other minorities, but it is not everyone's story or circumstances.

Here is how you can be an active ally to someone like me...

The short answer would be to listen and learn. Be willing to admit that you might have been wrong and accept that even our Scandinavian context is connected to a global, historical and political conversation.

2
HONEST INTROSPECTION

*"Knowing yourself is the
beginning of all wisdom"*
ARISTOTLE, *Greek philosopher and
polymath in Ancient Greece*

Let us begin this chapter with a visualisation.

Imagine that you are hosting a party to celebrate a significant event in your life. It could be a milestone birthday, a promotion, or a new educational qualification you have recently attained. You are dressed in your favourite outfit and feeling fabulous. Your home is all set up. The drinks are chilling, and the canapes are laid out. Your favourite music is softly playing in the background, and you have your drink of choice in your hand. The doorbell rings and you open the door to welcome your guests.

Who are the people that you have invited to your party?

Are they your friends, colleagues, or perhaps a mix of both? Would they have the same gender-identity and sexual orientation as you? Are they of a similar age, height and weight? How similar are their educational, cultural, and socio-economic backgrounds to yours? Do they tend to have similar views as you do on social and political matters? How similar are their personalities? Do they have a career in similar industries? Are their physical abilities similar to yours? Do they share the same beliefs and practices? What about their marital and parenthood choices? How similar are they to your own?

Can you see the cookie cutter?

We often choose to be friends and work with people who are similar to us; this phenomenon is known as *affinity bias*. While affinity bias is only one form of bias - there are indeed many others - what is bias to begin with?

Biases are our inclinations - stereotypes or prejudices - for or against a person or group, in a way that is considered to be unfair. Biases are developed over time through our early family and educational experiences, the culture and history of the society we grew up in, and then through our adult life experiences. We are all *socially conditioned* - the sociological process of training individuals in a society to respond in a manner generally approved by the society and by peer groups within society - to hold these biases. Teachers and nurses are female. Scientists and engineers are male. Skydiving and adrenaline sports are for the able and young. These implicit associations are created and compounded by what we see, hear and experience around us. In the 1980s and even 1990s, washing detergent commercials usually involved a frustrated woman, often a mother, with dirty and stained laundry in front of her. In walked a man, often a White man in a white coat - assumed to be a scientist - who had the answer: a washing detergent which would magically remove that stain. Social conditioning like the example above deepens the associations we have. *Discrimination* refers to behaviours that treat people unequally because of their group memberships. Discriminatory behaviour, ranging from insults to hate crimes, often begins with negative stereotypes and prejudices.

A *stereotype* is a specific belief, image or distorted truth about a person or group. It is a generalisation that allows for little or no individual differences or social variation. Stereotypes are based on images in mass media, or reputations passed on by parents, peers and other members of society. What is interesting is that stereotypes can be positive or negative. Closely related but a term to be understood in its own right, a *prejudice* is an opinion, prejudgment or attitude about a group or its individual members. A prejudice can be positive, but usually refers to a negative attitude. Prejudices are often accompanied by ignorance, fear or hatred. Prejudices are formed by a complex psychological process that begins with attachment to a close circle of acquaintances or an "in-group", and a prejudice is often aimed at the "out-groups". For example, Priya thinks that vegans are healthy and animal-loving while Ade thinks that meat eaters are strong given all the animal protein they consume. These are positive stereotypes. On the other hand, Priya also thinks that vegans are pedantic and think that they're better than everyone else while Ade thinks that meat eaters don't care about the environment. These are negative stereotypes. If Mary does not like David on the basis of David eating meat, that would be a negative prejudice.

In some of my corporate training sessions, I am confronted by participants - usually, though not always, White men - who question the idea that everyone is biased. They do so in defensiveness, and on the basis that they think that they are not racist, sexist, ageist or ableist. They assume that if one is biased, they must be racist, sexist, ageist or ableist. This is an incorrect assumption; a stereotype. If you are racist, sexist, ageist and ableist, you are indeed biased. However, having biases does not necessarily make you racist, sexist, ageist or ableist.

Here is the reality we have to come to terms with: If you have a brain, you are biased. Each of us has biases. Everyone. Even those of us who may think we are not biased absolutely are.

Accepting this truth and through honest introspection, we can allow ourselves to discover and unpack our biases. The challenge is that while there are indeed biases that we are aware of - our conscious biases - there are plenty of other biases we are unaware of - our unconscious biases. Biases are held by each one of us as individuals, and we also hold biases as teams and even collectively as organisations. Biases are also deeply embedded into the systems and processes in our organisations. These biases result in the cookie cutters we use as individuals, as teams and as organisations.

Our brains receive an extraordinary amount of information - 11 million bits of information every, single second.[49] We consciously process about 40 bits of information per second. Not 4 million; not 400,000; not 40,000; just 40. This means the remaining 99.9% of information is covered by our unconscious mind. We use algorithms and heuristics - a kind of mental shortcut - that we have developed over time to help us make sense of the overwhelming amount of information coming our way. We use these mental shortcuts to help us interpret and predict the happenings in the world around us. Our brains connect dots and fill in gaps, extrapolate and make assumptions based on incomplete information or similarity to previously recognised patterns. To be efficient and conserve our mental energy, our brain fits new information into existing frameworks rather than reconstructing it from scratch every time we receive new information.

These mental shortcuts help us survive. Yes, survive. Imagine you are a cave person hunting for food. You come across a large animal. If you consciously processed the 11 million bits of information every second - the animal is from the cat family, is very large, has a mane, claws, etc. - you would likely end up being dinner. This same instinctive decision making helps us cross the road or avoid dangerous situations by choosing the more populated train carriage at night or avoiding a deserted lane.

The problem is that we use similar mental shortcuts or biases when we meet and interact with people. The information we receive is so cognitively overwhelming, we sort people into groups. To save time and effort we arrange these groups based on stereotypes, the cultural environment around us and our personal experiences. So, instead of meeting the whole diverse self of each person, we meet them in the boxes that we sort them into. The reality is that our unconscious thoughts occur between 200 to 400 milliseconds[50] before our conscious processes engage, and those unconscious categorisations have implications on the accuracy and fairness of our decision making. Princeton psychologists Janine Willis and Alexander Todorov, who conducted a study that was published in 2006, found "that all it takes is a tenth of a second to form an impression of a stranger from their face".[51] In fact, research shows us that it takes just seven seconds to form a more complete impression of someone[52] or to form a prejudice based on someone's appearance.[53] Within that short period of time, we assess if someone is competent, confident or weak, friend or foe, likeable or trustworthy based on how they look and their body language.[54]

Conscious or *unconscious biases* are also sometimes referred to as explicit or implicit biases. Conscious, or explicit biases, are biases in which we are aware of the prejudices and stereotypes we hold. Unconscious, or implicit biases, are just that, unconscious. They are deeply ingrained mental associations that comprise accidental, unintended, subtle, unexamined, and completely unconscious choices and judgements. These choices and judgements are made by everyone, all the time, without our awareness and control - making the recognition of them challenging. It is important to note that conscious and unconscious biases can be held not just individually but collectively as well. *Collective biases* are prejudices and stereotypes held by groups of people about other individuals or groups. The more homogeneous a group is, the greater the collective bias that can potentially exist. For example, a team may hold a collective bias that they should hire someone from the same industry or educational institution that they all came from. We also have *systemic biases* that are deeply embedded into workplace systems, structures and processes, which we will look at later on in this book.

Within the workplace environment, conscious and unconscious biases affect (1) the process of decision making and the outcome of that process, (2) how we lead and manage other people in the workplace - people reporting to us, our colleagues and those we report to, and (3) our relationships with others - how we communicate, provide feedback and handle conflict.

Now that we know what biases are and established that we are all indeed biased, what can each one of us do to become more conscious of our biases? Keep in mind that we will never be completely free of bias; the way our brain works means that we will always use some degree of heuristics and algorithms to save time and keep us safe and free from danger.

What we can do is engage in honest introspection to become more aware of our biases and ensure that those biases do not seep into how we think, what we say, the decisions we make and what we do. As a starting point, it can be beneficial to do an Implicit Association Test.[55] However, we should not stop there. While such a test can help us identify and understand what our unconscious biases might be at a theoretical level, to truly be aware of our unconscious biases requires sincere reflection and introspection. As I often say to the audiences in my keynote sessions, it has taken us decades to pack on our biases nice and thick, it will take us time and significant effort to unpack them.

During a bias awareness workshop for a large FMCG company, a participant shared his reflection. At the end of the workday, he often asks colleagues to join him for a drink at the pub. While this was coming from a place of wanting to socialise and get to know each other better, he hadn't thought that it was excluding others - colleagues who don't drink alcohol and those who have to pick up their children or care for their elderly parents. At that session, he committed to making an effort to be more inclusive. Since then, he has organised hikes, brunches/dinners, and walking tours of the city at different times and days of the week to cater for the diversity of his colleagues.

To help us with unpacking our biases, the rest of this chapter contains a number of different exercises to help you engage in honest introspection and discover more about yourself and how you interact with others. Changing our behaviours begins with understanding ourselves better; this helps us connect the dots between our biases and what we say and do. Honest introspection helps us identify the gap between where we are now and where we would like to be. While most of these exercises require you to work individually, some of them have the option of engaging with members of your team as well. If biases are learned, it is time to unlearn them, and that requires honest introspection.

Honest introspection means:

- Coming to terms with and accepting that you are biased.
- Understanding that everyone has biases.
- Realising that biases are systemic and deeply embedded in the ways in which things are done.
- Reflecting on your own biases - the conscious ones but also where the unconscious ones could lie.
- Becoming more aware of and recognising biases around you.

I am...but I am not ...

This exercise can be done on your own or with a colleague, friend or partner, or even as a team at the start of your next meeting or off-site.

Fill in the following sentence: I am _____ but I am not _____.

Come up with as many of these sentences as you can within a few minutes. It may feel challenging to do this, but it is an integral process into learning more about ourselves, the boxes into which society and others put us into and our own struggles with defining who we are. In doing so, my hope is that you also become aware of the boxes or cookie cutters that others are also put into or forced to conform to.

Let me share some of my statements:
I am someone with curly hair, but I am not unprofessional.
I am ethnically Indian, but I am not in IT.
I am a South Asian woman, but I am not only a wife and mother.
I am cisgender, but I am not transphobic.
I am an Associate Professor, but I am not anti-social.
I am a public speaker, but I am not extroverted.
I am ethnically Indian, but I am not from India.
I am a South Asian woman, but I am not voiceless.

....
....
....
....
....
....
....
....
....
....
....
....
....
....
....
....
....
....
....
....
....
....
....
....

Optional: Once you are done with your own sentences, you can share them with others and listen to theirs. This exercise can be very powerful to do in a team to unearth some of those false assumptions that we make about each other.

My biases: Where do they lie?

While we find it very hard to accept that we are biased, we are. Even those who experience bias against themselves, have biases against others. We *all* have biases. So where do our biases lie? Here is a list of common biases or -isms that are experienced in our workplaces. Reflect on where your biases may lie. If you are feeling courageous, put a tick next to the ones which you recognise as your bias, and write down a specific way or incident in which your thoughts, words, decisions or actions reflect the bias. Remember, we all have biases across most, if not all, of these forms of bias.

☐ Sexism: Biases and discrimination on the basis of sex and gender.

....
....
....
....

☐ Homophobia/Heterosexism/Transphobia: Biases and discrimination on the basis of a person's sexual orientation or gender identity.

....
....
....
....

☐ Ageism: Biases and discrimination against a person's age.

....

....

....

....

☐ Ableism: Biases and discrimination against people with disabilities based on the belief that typical abilities are superior.

....

....

....

....

☐ Lookism/Heightism/Weightism/Hairism: Biases and discrimination on the basis on how a person looks/their height/their weight/ their natural hair.

....

....

....

....

☐ Education-ism: Biases and discrimination of the basis of a person's educational qualifications and where they attained that qualification from.

....

....

....

....

☐ Experience-ism: Biases and discrimination based on the work and life experiences that someone has. For example, having a criminal record or having a military background.

....

....

....

☐ Personality-ism: Biases and discrimination favouring certain personality types for certain roles.

....

....

....

☐ Neurodiversity-ism: Biases and discrimination on the basis of different ways of thinking and learning towards people who have dyslexia, dyspraxia, autism, Asperger's and attention deficit hyperactivity disorder (ADHD).

....

....

....

☐ Racism/Colourism: Biases and discrimination against people on the basis of their membership in a particular racial or ethnic group, typically one that is an under-represented or marginalised.

....

....

....

....

☐ Foodism: Biases and discrimination on the basis of people's food choices due to health, sustainability or religious reasons.

....

....

☐ Religion-ism: Biases and discrimination on the basis of people's religious beliefs and practices, including clothing and symbols.

....

....

....

☐ Accentism: Biases and discrimination on the basis of the way a language is spoken, usually by non-native speakers.

....

....

....

☐ Marital/Parenthood-ism: Biases and discrimination on the basis on people's marital and parenthood choices.

....

....

....

☐ Background-ism: Biases and discrimination on the basis of a person's socio-economic background.

....

....

....

How do my biases form?

We are all socially conditioned. This social conditioning contributes to our biases. Our life experiences have shaped us and our world view.

For the biases you have reflected on in the previous exercise 'My biases: Where do they lie?', reflect on where those biases likely come from using the list below. How have these factors played a role in the biases you hold? How have they influenced you to think, speak and act the way you do? Be honest and go deep.

- ☐ Family
- ☐ Culture
- ☐ History
- ☐ Where you have lived
- ☐ Education
- ☐ Work industry/company/experience
- ☐ Partners & children
- ☐ Friends
- ☐ Media
- ☐ Politics
- ☐ Socio-economic background
- ☐ Others?

....

....

My inclusion journey

Now that we have had some time to reflect on our biases, the next step is to focus on making sense of inclusion. We feel inclusion, and the lack of, and everyone's inclusion journey - even in the same environment - is different. The first step in understanding this journey is to reflect on it.

1. Look back on your life. Reflect on the key events in your life where you felt included and times when you did not.
2. Identify 7-10 events during your life when you felt included and when you did not. If you are having difficulty, imagine that you are producing a movie about your life's experience with inclusion. What would the main scenes be?
3. Divide the horizontal axis of the graph on the next page into appropriate equal time intervals representing your life. For example, if you are 45 years old, then put 5 markings down each indicating a 10-year period.
4. For each event when you felt included, put a cross mark [X] above the dotted line to indicate where in time that event occurred and how inclusive that event was for you. Then label or name the event. Identify what conditions were present for each of those cross marks. You can use the list provided to help you.
5. For each event when you felt un-included, put a cross mark [X] above the dotted line to indicate where in time that event occurred and how non-inclusive that event was for you. Then label or name the event. Identify what conditions were absent for each of those cross marks. You can use the list provided to help you.

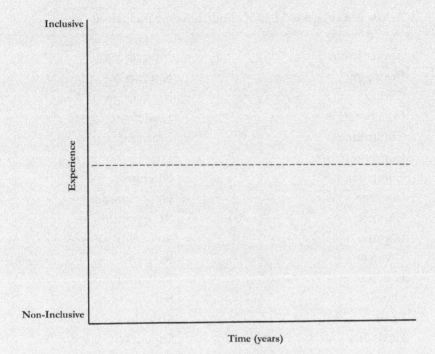

Rank the top 5 conditions you chose that you believe are most important for inclusion to exist from the ones that you used in mapping your journey. These reflect the conditions needed for you to feel included. They are unique to you. When these conditions are met, or most are, you feel inclusion.

1. ....

2. ....

3. ....

4. ....

5. ....

Below is a suggested list of conditions for inclusion:

Appreciation

Belonging

Caring

Collaboration

Commitment

Community

Compassion

Courage

Curiosity

Dignity

Diversity

Equality

Equity

Faith

Flexibility

Friendship

Fun

Gratitude

Growth

Honesty

Humility

Independence

Integrity

Kindness

Knowledge

Leadership

Learning

Love

Openness

Opportunities

Recognition

Reliability

Respect

Responsibility

Socialisation

Structure

Support

Tradition

Trust

Understanding

Value

Well-being

Wholeheartedness

Others? Write them here:

....

....

....

....

....

....

What does the cookie cutter look like at work?

Think about the people that you work with. You could think about your colleagues, your managers or leaders, or those reporting to you. How similar are they to each other? Reflect on the similarities in the following dimensions: their gender, sexual orientation, age, abilities, appearances, educational background, personality, life and professional experiences, ways of communicating, thinking and learning, ethnicity and culture, beliefs and practices, marital and parenthood choices and their socio-economic background.

Write these similarities down in the cookie cutter below. Be honest. It may feel uncomfortable to come to terms with the cookie cutter, but they exist.

Understanding what the cookie cutter looks like is an important step in honest introspection. Once we know what the mould looks like, we can then take actions to reshape it; to expand it or even melt it down.

Prachi Thakur (She/Her)

I am a young Indian female, born in Bihar, India's second most illiterate state, in an underprivileged family. I also have visible tattoos and piercings which are an important aspect of how I see myself.

My story here is based on the following intersectional dimensions of diversity: Gender - Age - Socio-economic background - Physical appearances (Visible tattoos and multiple piercings)

Here is my story of bias and discrimination...

Since I grew up in a household where I had no female siblings, I have faced discrimination at multiple fronts since my childhood. My grandmother was a typically patriarchal lady who never wanted a female child in the first place. My mother shares that when my elder brother was born, my grandmother sent toys and gifts, but when I was born, she sent nothing. Throughout my childhood, she kept tormenting me by blaming me for every wrong thing that ever happened. If someone fell down, they must have seen my face in the morning; if someone tripped, I must have crossed their path; if I fell down, I don't know how to walk; when my brother fell down, I must have pushed him. You get the idea: there was nothing I could ever do right!

My grandmother wanted me to get married when she was on the death bed in 2009. At that time, I was in grade 9, around 13 years old. It wouldn't have been an odd thing to do since many of my friends were getting married around that time, but I never wanted to. It was my elder brother who stood up for me, like a wall to prevent that from happening.

Throughout school, people teased me for the status we had - none. My father repairs cooking stoves for a living, so we weren't the most "maintained" students in school. Our clothes would be clean, but often with stitches and faded stains. I wore my brother's trousers throughout my schooling. For most kids in my school, a new school year meant new notebooks. Not for me. People didn't invite me to birthday parties because I couldn't invite them back. We never had birthday parties in my family.

When I was doing my Masters degree, I started travelling. Travelling was a whole new world for a person like me - a person who had never travelled for leisure. However, traveling was a whole new world for discrimination as well. The most important moment, which also became the pivoting point in my life, was the one in the Indian city of Varanasi. It was a winter evening, and I was waiting at a hotel gate for my cab to arrive. The desk receptionist commented "You won't be back tonight, will you?". He assumed that because of my tattoos, I must be a sex worker and that the night was when I worked! That moment pushed me to do something to change the way we see tattoos and women.

Here is how you can be an active ally to someone like me...

Don't associate someone's financial condition with their value, and don't pity them. There have been cases where I have been pitied and it's an absolutely horrible feeling. I have never understood why people pity someone in the first place. In my opinion, if you can't say/do something to be helpful, keep quiet.

As an ally, don't equate age with brilliance, and age is definitely not equal to knowledgeability. I have trained senior executives of respected hotel chains, and they have written me notes of appreciation for my work. People should understand that I might be young, but that's the thing. I am young so I bring a perspective to the table that others never can!

Tattoos and piercings are personal things. Before you ask someone about their tattoos, ask them if they are comfortable talking about it.

Your first question to me should never be any of the following:

What does your tattoo mean?
Where did you get your tattoo?
Oh, I can never get a tattoo!
Didn't it hurt?
Why did you get a tattoo?
Which language is this?
Where did you get it?

Did your parents know about it?
Will you get a job with these?

If you do, be prepared to receive sarcastic and disrespectful answers. If you absolutely have to ask someone about their tattoos, here are some questions you can use:

Hey, your tattoo looks beautiful, may I ask you something about it if you're comfortable?
Hello, I was curious about your beautiful tattoo, and was wondering if you are comfortable answering some questions about it?

There should always be a compliment + your intention + asking about my comfort level.

My gender identity should not be equated with what I can or cannot do. I have come across so many people who ask me questions around:

"Oh, your English is pretty good for someone from Bihar."
"Do your parents know you travel this much?"
"How do your parents allow you to travel this much?"
"How do you fund your travel?"
"How do you not feel afraid as a girl?"

Learn how to be respectful, and mind your own business when you meet someone. If you are curious about something I do, follow the drill above: compliment + your intention + asking about my comfort level.

Sarah Freiesleben (She/Her)

A few years back, I found it nearly impossible to continue working in the corporate world due to the short-sightedness of the leadership surrounding and constraining me. I resigned and started my own company, wanting to do things differently, but I also wanting to hide. The ubiquitous need others seemed to have for me to be either a specialist or a generalist and colour within the lines, while talking about "innovation" and "transformation", had taken its toll on me. I wanted to combine unexpected things, adjust constraints causing dilemmas, and create new paths. I sought help from therapy and comforted myself with deep intellectual pursuits in systems theory and cybernetics.

Eventually, it came to my attention that my way of thinking and having the world respond to you, is common among autistic people. It made sense and I began identifying as such, finding the pathology served as a helpful sensemaking shortcut to help others understand me, in hopes that this understanding would help the world accept me. However, I soon

found the label of autism to be its own restrictive box, reducing my iden-
tity which is complex and contextual, to a static description. And came to
find that what is useful to help us make sense of ourselves or each other,
can become harmful when it is seen as one's complete identity, of which
everything we think or do is an effect.

The more I shared my story, the more I realized everyone's identity is
comprised of various ever evolving parts; we just have varying degrees of
conscious acceptance of this. At the time of writing this I refer to autism
as one way to make sense of some of me. In a few years' time, I may read
this and not identify with it at all.

My story here is based on the following intersectional dimensions
of diversity: Gender – Experiences, skills, & Interests - Personality -
Neurodiversity

Here is my story of bias and discrimination...

In my life, I have encountered often extreme reactions to my way of
being but have struggled to explain these encounters. Since I am always
part of the interaction, it is always easy to blame myself for being too
vocal; for bringing up things other people find irrelevant, but I see a
connection in; for pointing out too many awkward truths; or for just
being different from how people expect me to be. But I have come to
realize that these encounters are neither about me, nor about people
discriminating against me; they are relational. I hope my stories can
shed light on nuances that we all can contribute to improving together.

Once, I was aggressively fired by my manager at an offsite team
building event. I sensed that his actions were triggered by the combination of me being a woman, scoring a "D" on the DISC profile that day,

and being selected for a promotion by his manager, against his wishes. I could not prove this, and the man found the suggestion of my gender as a factor preposterous since he "had never been accused of being sexist before." I was not accusing him of being sexist though. There was something unique in the dynamic between us, of which only one influencing part was my gender. Perhaps it was my own embodiment of my gender, along with all its historical insecurities that triggered me to recognize how it mattered in our interactions. His need to talk about his achievements, searching for a reaction; the subtle disappointments I could see in his eyes when he did not find the reaction he wanted; his comments about how he did not expect to see (someone like) me eating a hotdog; subtle things. The HR department and leadership, who had recently promoted me, did not even offer to hear my side of the story. I was treated like a criminal as I returned my laptop and phone. This was the same week the corporate HR department was wrangling up women to take pictures for LinkedIn about their focus on diversity. I have no doubt they wanted more women in their IT department. But did they want women like me?

Part of my autism "diagnosis" has been shadowed by scoring high on intelligence tests, as there are many crossovers between being "gifted" and being "autistic". I have always been able to sense that there is more than my gender at play in the negative reactions I encounter in the world. For example, I have had numerous men who work with innovation react aggressively towards me for using words they did not understand. They accuse me of trying to "seem smarter than they", show off, or lecture them. I am usually working on the assumption that people who work in innovation are curious and want to engage in mutual learning, but I seem to trigger their insecurities. They react to me as if I have intended to make them feel small, but I see these same men engaging with curiosity with men who act similarly to me. We have a nutty professor architype that allows people to feel comfortable with their quirky ideas and larger lexicon.

The most insidious form of bias that I feel is related to the variation of my interests, skills, & ideas. I have an advanced degree in the humanities yet work in technology; and have worked across several industries, with almost all corporate functions. People often see this as me being indecisive, but the variation is purposeful. In my free time I read novels & about all sorts of things: anthropology, philosophy, math, religion, war, mindfulness, technology, AI, leadership, ethics, etc. and enjoy inspirations found at the intersections between all of it. I listen to all sorts of music and have a very hard time answering survey & personality test questions because my favourite & often missing answer is "all of the above". But recently I was called "incoherent" by someone whom I had politely asked about their exclusion of me. My greatest strength, blending and playing with possibilities between things, was an inconvenience to his process. People who identify as "pragmatic" often see me as their enemy. Little do they know that once I am finished diverging, I am a convergence master, often creating much more practical solutions than they do.

Here is how you can be an active ally to someone like me...

The best way you can be an ally to me is to genuinely accept the multiplicity of me. Sometimes I am introverted, sometimes extroverted. Sometimes I go deep when you want to go broad, or I go adjacent when you may want to go deep. Let us explore & guide each other. You may tell me I overthink things, and you will not be wrong; I have low latent inhibition (look it up). My wish is that you navigate your difficulty to make sense of me from a place of curiosity instead of judgement. There is a chance that if you find me over-complicated, I find you over-simplistic. I also commit to respect and strive to understand your ways of being.

I have learned that finding acceptance from others starts with deep inquiry and acceptance of our true selves. My wish is that we all show up with agency & freedom to be our continuously evolving and multi-faceted selves, without having to put a label on each beautiful nuance, ready to meet each other with respect and appreciation for this variety. It is, after all, what fuels our evolution.

3
HUMBLE ACKNOWLEDGEMENT

"We come nearest to the great when we are great in humility."

RABINDRANATH TAGORE, *the first non-European writer to be awarded the Nobel Prize for Literature*

The world is not experienced in the same way by everyone. That is the hard reality we must come to terms with by humbly acknowledging that we don't know or fully comprehend how life is experienced by someone else.

As human beings, we have a tendency to assume that the world is experienced in exactly the same way by everyone - in a cookie cutter kind of way. In cultures where equality is really valued and forms an integral part of people's mindset and values, this can be even more prevalent. In the Nordic countries, one cannot ignore the influence of the Law of Jante,[56] which expands on the theme: *You are not to think you are anyone special or that you are better than us.* The ten rules that comprise the law come from a novel written in 1933 by Danish-Norwegian author Aksel Sandemose. These laws have had a profound influence on nurturing the sense of equality the region is so well known for. The rules act as a self-correcting mechanism where people feel uncomfortable with even the slightest hint of inequality that they see or think of themselves, and very swiftly seek to "come back to being equal". This self-correcting mechanism has some advantages to maintaining a sense of equality in workplaces and society. However, if it seems almost too good to be true, there is a dark side. These rules can also create a *positivity bias*, where people assume that everyone sees everyone else as equal, and that the world is experienced in the very same way by everyone else. While on the surface this might not seem like a bad thing, it can in fact act as a barrier to acknowledging the very existence of inequality.

As an example, I was recently speaking at an event for a large Nordic Pharmaceutical company. After my keynote address, we had the opportunity to engage in a question-and-answer session. A participant shared that the idea of equity makes her feel uncomfortable; that someone might be given additional resources or opportunities not given to someone else. I was glad she felt psychologically safe enough to raise this with me and her colleagues. She continued to explain that when she was a child, she had to share whatever she had equally with her siblings. If she had an apple, she had to share it in equal parts with them. She recounted that she had the same educational opportunities as her brothers. I listened and acknowledged her experience. I then shared a different picture. In some parts of the world where poverty is the norm, when a parent can afford only one glass of milk, that glass is often given to the male child. The female child receives very little or nothing. The world is not experienced the same way by everyone. That may be hard to accept, but it is the truth. Take a moment and let that sink in.

When you are ready, think about whether you have had to:

- Justify your entry into a country.
- Explain and defend where you are from and/or answer the follow-up question: Where you are *actually* from?
- Alter your hair to be seen as professional.
- Make considered choices about what to wear to be taken seriously.
- Hide who you love out of fear of judgement or worse, criminal persecution.
- Alter or even change your name.
- Downplay your invisible disabilities to get an interview.
- Go through additional rounds of job interviews.
- Be declined a job on the basis of "not fitting in".

How many of the above don't apply to you or your experiences? The ones you have not had to think about form the basis of your privilege. Scholar and activist Peggy McIntosh defines privilege as the "invisible, weightless knapsack of special advantages carried by persons native to the majority, but denied to those who form the minority."[57] Privilege can stem from any single or combination of, but not limited to, the following sources:

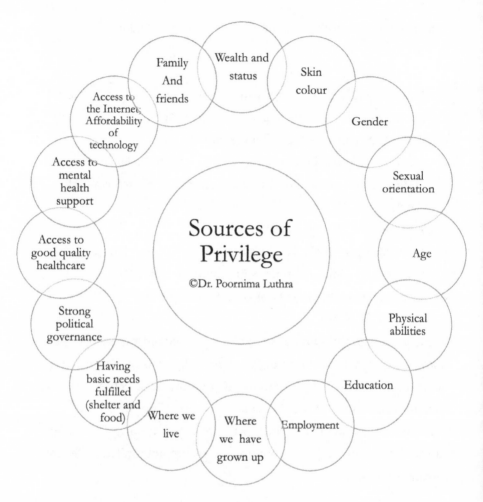

Sources of privilege

Our privilege stems from all the biases and experiences of discrimination we have not experienced in life, but that others have had to navigate. Many who belong to a represented group - those who "fit" the cookie cutter - don't see these as issues because they don't experience them. This is a challenge we must address. Just because something does not affect you or you don't experience it does not mean that it doesn't exist. Privilege is assuming something is not a problem because it is not a problem for *you*.

Acknowledging privilege is recognising that the race track of life looks and feels different for everyone. For some the race track may be clear of obstacles. For others there are small pebbles they need to jump over. For some there are larger rocks or even boulders. For still others, there may be hills or mountains blocking their way altogether.

Privilege is a loaded word these days. In my DEI workshops, things can get uncomfortable (and that is a good thing). Questions often come up, such as "Why should I feel guilty for being White?", "Why should I feel guilty for the privileges that come from being male?" or "I didn't ask to be born this way, why should I feel guilty about it?"

Acknowledging one's privilege means recognising that your circumstances and situation play a crucial role in defining your experiences. Acknowledging one's privilege is about nurturing empathy, not defensiveness. It is about recognising that the paths we take are different, depending on whether we come from a represented or under-represented group. Those from represented groups are less likely to have experienced racism, sexism, ageism or ableism, or if they have, not to the same extent as those from under-represented, marginalised or discriminated groups. That is the privilege one has.

Many of us have some degree of privilege, some more than others. Awareness of privilege means acknowledging the existence of systemic biases and discrimination towards some and not others. The ability to empathise with someone who has experienced discrimination acknowledges that the world is indeed not equal, and our experiences, even of the same context, are different. Those who are unable to demonstrate empathy or acknowledge privilege are the biggest roadblocks to inclusion. In the words of American professor, author and podcast host,

Brené Brown: "Avoiding difficult conversations is the definition of privilege."

To understand the situation we are in today where some have privilege and others don't, we need to look to history - to the role of colonialism, supremacy, and slavery. The purpose of history should be to remind us why we are where we are today, to provide context and legitimacy to the experience of those who have been discriminated against, and to remind us not to repeat those mistakes again. We need to confront history so we make things better but we also need to confront all of history - the good, the bad and the ugly. Yet, we live in a world where certain groups do not want parts of history to be talked about or taught to children. In the US, the heated national debate about teaching critical race theory to school children is one such example. Critical race theory (CRT) is an academic concept that emerged in the late 1970s and 1980s based on the work of legal scholars Derrick Bell, Kimberlé Crenshaw, and Richard Delgado, among others. The core idea is that race is a social construct, and that racism is not merely the product of individual bias or prejudice, but also something embedded in legal systems and policies. The theory says that racism is part of everyday life, so people - White or non-White - who don't intend to be racist can nevertheless make choices that propagate racism. Critics of critical race theory believe that it discriminates against White people in order to further the goal of equity. But by lumping everything race-related under the label of CRT, we are being given an inaccurate version of history. I believe that it's important that we do not fight bias with further bias, but not at the expense of false narratives about what discrimination looks like today or in the past.

We must come to terms with history. We must humbly acknowledge the mistakes of the past. We must sit with the discomfort of those truths no matter how uncomfortable it feels. Only when we do this can we move forward. At the same time, we should use our privilege to learn how to be more active allies, and active allyship needs humble acknowledgment. In the words of the American author and social activist bell hooks, "Privilege is not in and of itself bad; what matters is what we do with privilege...Privilege does not have to be negative, but we have to share our resources and take direction about how to use our privilege in ways that empower those who lack it."

Humble acknowledgement means:

- Accepting that life is not experienced by others in the same way as you.
- Being able to say "I don't know or fully comprehend how life is experienced by someone else."
- Reflecting on where your privilege lies with the intention of harnessing that knowledge to be an active ally.
- Listening to and empathising with others' life stories with a desire to understand life experiences of biases and discrimination that may be unfamiliar to you, without dismissing their experiences as being unusual or not "normal".
- Always asking if there is someone better able to share their experiences of bias and discrimination than you, so that the other person/people/audience feel heard and seen.

Owning my privilege

Where does your privilege lie? What have you NOT had to think about/ worry about/stress about in life? Those are your privileges. In my book *Diversifying Diversity*, I write: "In order for us to walk in someone else's shoes, we must first take off our own."[58]

Take a look at the sources of privilege below and mark the ones where you believe you have privilege. Remember that privilege is not something to fear. We need to embrace privilege, and by doing so it allows us to build empathy by helping us humbly acknowledge that the race track of life looks different for us all.

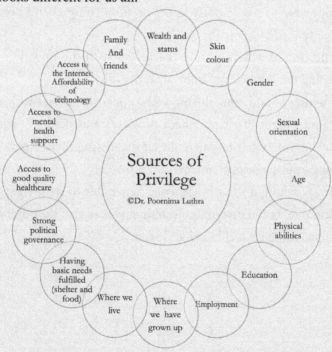

Diving deeper into privilege

Below are a set of statements. If you agree with the statements, tick the box next to it.

- ☐ The leaders in my company are mostly people of my gender. The higher up in the corporate hierarchy, the more this is true.
- ☐ My leadership skills or work abilities are not questioned by others based on my gender.
- ☐ My manager is a person of my gender.
- ☐ When completing surveys/forms for work, my gender is an option on the drop-down menu.
- ☐ I do not have to worry about being interrupted during meetings.
- ☐ It is extremely rare that someone explains things to me in a way that makes me feel less competent.
- ☐ It is rare that someone takes my ideas during a meeting, reshares them and gains greater acceptance of the idea than when I shared my ideas.
- ☐ I am not told that I am in the "wrong" restroom.
- ☐ I do not worry that if people know my sexual orientation and/or gender identity there will be emotional, physical, or psychological consequences.
- ☐ I can marry my partner legally, and receive work benefits for my spouse and myself.
- ☐ I can bring my partner to a company event without concern of being judged or treated differently.

☐ No one believes my sexual orientation and/or gender identity was "caused" by sin, disease, or abuse.

☐ I have never been refused an opportunity or job because of my age.

☐ It is rare that people dismiss my view citing that I am "too young" or "lacking life experience" because of my age.

☐ I have never been refused a job because "there were many other applicants with much more experience."

☐ I have never been made fun of or mocked for not knowing something current.

☐ Others don't assume I don't know things simply because of my age.

☐ I can easily get into any building or room that I need to enter.

☐ I have never been stared at, or been left out, due to a disability.

☐ People do not treat me as if I am less capable of doing my work because of the look or ability of my body.

☐ Strangers do not ask me what happened to my body.

☐ Workplaces and work tools do not have to be modified to meet my needs.

☐ I do not have to alter my natural hair to be seen to be professional.

☐ I do not have to carefully choose what I wear to ensure that I am taken seriously.

☐ The leaders in my company and I are about the same height.

☐ I have never felt judged because of my weight.

☐ I have never felt that I have not gotten a job or promotion because of my weight.

☐ My educational background is viewed as prestigious.

☐ I am rarely asked questions about why I made the educational choices I did.

☐ I do not have a criminal record.

☐ I have never been told that my personality is unsuitable for a job.

- ☐ The ways in which I think and learn are considered "normal".
- ☐ I am comfortable looking at others in their eyes.
- ☐ Open offices do not bother me.
- ☐ I grew up in the country I currently live in.
- ☐ I am never stopped at immigration queues when travelling for work because of my nationality.
- ☐ I have never felt judged or had people give me suspicious looks because of my skin colour.
- ☐ I can usually find people of my ethnic background in top management and leadership roles in my organisation.
- ☐ The official language of my company is one that I am fluent in.
- ☐ My accent is well understood by my colleagues, and I am rarely asked to repeat myself because of it.
- ☐ I have never felt like hiding or changing my name/surname.
- ☐ I can go shopping alone most of the time, being sure that I will not be followed or closely watched by store employees because of my ethnic background.
- ☐ I can take a job with an employer who believes in equal opportunity employment without others thinking that I got my job only because of my ethnic background.
- ☐ I have never felt like the "token" hire.
- ☐ I have never been the first person of my ethnicity to be hired to my team or organisation.
- ☐ I can be fairly sure that I will not have to work on the religious holidays that are important to me.
- ☐ Most of my managers and colleagues are familiar with my faith.
- ☐ Food that does not violate my religious or environmental beliefs can be easily found in the office canteen and at work-related events.
- ☐ I do not need to explain my food choices to others.

- ☐ Most people do not consider my religious practices to be "weird" or "old-fashioned".
- ☐ I do not need to worry about how I would be judged by wearing clothing or symbols of my religion to work.
- ☐ My marital choices are rarely met with disapproval.
- ☐ I am rarely asked when I will have a baby.
- ☐ During the COVID-19 pandemic, I did not have to juggle work and childcare responsibilities/home learning for my children. Someone else was the primary caregiver for my children.
- ☐ I outsource childcare responsibilities to my partner or spouse.
- ☐ I work for a company with parenthood policies for my gender.
- ☐ I am not penalised for using my company's parenthood policies.
- ☐ If I have children and a successful career, I am rarely asked how I manage to balance my professional and private lives.
- ☐ My parents went to college/university.
- ☐ I grew up in a house with many books.
- ☐ My parents have been able to help me with writing job/college applications.
- ☐ The majority of the kids in the area(s) where I grew up went to college/university.
- ☐ I have never been homeless.
- ☐ I have never had to skip a meal to save money.
- ☐ During the COVID-19 pandemic, I had easy access to technology and the Internet.
- ☐ During the COVID-19 pandemic, I had enough space to work at home.
- ☐ I have a family whom I go home to every evening.
- ☐ I have health insurance and access to good quality healthcare.
- ☐ I have easy access to mental health care should I need it.
- ☐ I live in a country with a strong and stable political system.

How are you feeling after completing this? Reflect on the statements that you ticked; those are the things you don't need to think about that others do. They are where your privilege lies. Compare these with your response to the previous exercise 'Owning my Privilege'. Think about the statements you did not tick. What surprised you most as you read these statements? What have you learnt about yourself?

....
....
....
....
....
....
....
....
....
....
....
....
....
....
....
....
....
....
....
....
....
....

Se-Hsieng Eng (She/Her)

I am a Singaporean woman in technology of ethnic Chinese origin and a mother of two adolescent boys. I was born and raised in Singapore. I had never travelled abroad before a school field trip to Bali and Darwin when I was 15 years old. The next time I left my country, I was heading to Paris for 2 years to complete my double degree in engineering. Thereafter, I worked in Manila and London for large tele- communications companies with ample opportunities to fly to Pakistan, the UAE, Oman, Cameroon, South Africa and multiple Western Euro- pean cities for business. Since 2019, I have been based in Singapore as part of the global management team for a technology start-up.

My story here is based on the following intersectional dimensions of diversity: Personality - Race, ethnicity and culture - Marital and parenthood choices - Socio-economic background

Here is my story of bias and discrimination...

I think I have been fortunate - a word that is common in my ethnic Chinese Singaporean culture - but as I use the word, I realise that I should not completely discount the efforts put in to overcome biases, discriminations or unpleasant situations along the way in my career. For example, when I first volunteered for a long-term overseas assignment in a "less-developed country", I was told I would be mad "as a lady" to volunteer for a "difficult" posting. Through mutual collaboration and persistence, I finally became the first female engineer assigned as Head of Cost Control in one of our overseas affiliates in South-East Asia for a period of twelve months.

My reasons for requesting that first assignment were simple. Firstly, I had been in a long-term relationship and knew we were likely to get married and build a family together one day. I desperately wanted to have the experience of working overseas before our family would expand. Secondly, I felt strongly that I would be able to contribute internationally given my prior tertiary education experience in France. Without allies, I would not have been able to embark on this journey. My superiors and HR finally agreed to allow me to switch departments laterally, in order to spend a year learning precise skills deemed to be more relevant for the overseas affiliates. Was this an ambitious approach? Perhaps. I saw it as a natural and pragmatic path for a young adult woman who wanted to maximise professional learning opportunities in tandem with personal family goals.

The journey was not always smooth. I often talk about the times when I was on international work trips as a new mother. I frequently had to express breastmilk to freeze for my young baby back home, yet it was challenging to find female toilets, much less clean breastfeeding facilities, on the board-room floor of a large telecommunications firm.

The guard looked incredulously at me when I asked him for directions, and it soon became clear I would find the required conveniences only on the ground floor. At other times in various locations, it became necessary to use A4 sheets and sticky tape to block off the see-through windows found in the doors of office supply rooms in order to indicate I was not to be disturbed while expressing milk. I persisted through these challenges because I earnestly believed that motherhood should not get in the way of contributions and continuous learning at the workplace. It is certainly my hope that as we define the new normal of hybrid work environments and living with Covid-19, accommodations for new parents are taken into serious account in our urban planning and that the gift of life does not preclude other life choices.

A few years later, my husband and I discussed the possibility of exposing our two young boys to some of the international experiences we had previously encountered. We wondered if they would find living abroad as exciting and stimulating as we had, albeit at a much younger age. I again embarked on the wondrous journey of mapping out a 5-year work-life game plan – first convincing our loved ones and extended family at home of our readiness to move abroad for an extended period of time as a family unit, while my husband discussed potential sabbatical plans with his employer. With the buy-in from initial stakeholders, I then broached the topic with middle and senior management in my local division, overseas units at headquarters, local, regional and global human resource departments, as well as talent management units at the global telecommunications firm I was then working in, all of whom became precious allies and friends till this day. Working in the Asia-Pacific office meant I would naturally be considered for or made aware of either domestic or pan-Asian roles. In contrast, equivalent or more junior European counterparts based in headquarters were being offered international roles anywhere in the world with no prerequisites for prior cultural familiarity! Why was this? After eighteen months of proving myself through continued performance, influencing others across the ranks about my "adaptability" and strong allies giving ample assurances internally that my prior education in France and my INSEAD Executive MBA would arm me with the necessary "cross-cultural sensitivities", I was finally given the opportunity to lead a strategic technology sales unit based out of the London headquarters. It was the first time that the sales unit of over 60 colleagues in 9 countries would be led by a female of Asian origin in its history. My family and I gained countless precious memories and experiences from our time in the United Kingdom.

Finally, I guess my name is not an easy one to pronounce or even spell. But I take pride in it because it contains elements of my Teochew (Southern Chinese) heritage and signifies my forefathers' immigrant lineage in multicultural Singapore. My first name 'Se-Hsieng' has far too many vowels mangled up with a silent capital 'H' all thrown in. The last 3 letters resemble an alliteration of my last name 'Eng'. In the Philippines, I adopted the nickname Shereen, to avoid being called Ma'am all day at work. In London, I often used SH and even now in my birth country, I often shorten it to Hsieng. I do know my name is probably unique and not the only representation of who I am. Have I wondered if I might be passed over for some opportunities because of the complexity of maintaining a complex Asian-sounding name in a Western context? Perhaps. Nonetheless, I can always tell when someone puts in the effort to get my name right. I hope I bring the same level of respectful curiosity that I hope to get from others to new situations around me and people I meet.

Here is how you can be an active ally to someone like me...

Do practise active listening skills to build trust and rapport.

Do not interrupt unnecessarily - it will shake the confidence of the person and discourage further sharing.

Do not offer solutions before understanding the full personal and professional context in which the person is operating. Family circumstances, past history, childhood etc. are all likely to play a part in how a person is operating at the workplace.

Do support the person to hold space and reflect on any biases or discriminations that the person feels they have encountered and link how the facts made them feel. Often, they need support to get over the injustice of the situation before they can take stock and reflect on their takeaways and strengthen their resolve for the next step.

Do share examples from your own journey. But be sensitive that your own experience, especially of how you personally overcame certain hurdles, might not always be relevant. Instead, support the development of a relevant action plan with personal ownership and regular checkpoints.

Jessica Spence (She/Her)

I was born in the UK but grew up overseas and over the last 15 years, I have lived across Europe, Asia and the US, progressing in my career whilst also balancing my husband's. I am British by birth, but never really lived there and have always felt slightly "homeless" - in both positive and negative ways. Travelling and working across the world has given me a much deeper appreciation for the level of privilege I have had, and made me reflect on how much of what I have achieved can be put down to where I was born, the colour of my skin and the means my parents had to invest in me.

My story here is based on the following intersectional dimensions of diversity: Gender - Marital and parenthood choices

Here is my story of bias and discrimination...

I didn't realise I was managing biases and discrimination for probably about 20 years. I just didn't frame it as that. I framed it as "this is the way the world is". I was brought up by two wonderful parents who never questioned what I could (or couldn't) do. It was only when I reached college that I started to notice a few things but rationalised it away as "that's just how it is". When applying to colleges, I was advised not to apply to one college because "they only take one or two women and they are always blonde". When I wanted to take a class in aesthetics, I was told that the teacher wouldn't teach women. When I did some research for my student's union on why women got fewer First Class degrees, I was told that "well, does it really matter? After all, what do women need them for?" and "Maybe women's brains just aren't wired to get first class degrees". Both of these coming from the very people who were meant to teach, inspire and nurture these women. But I never framed this as "discrimination" - just the way things were.

At work it was more subtle; sometimes but not always. I was paid less than my male peers on the grounds that "my husband also worked so I didn't need as much money". I was removed from my role as the highest performing person in my peer group across several years by a leader who found me insufficiently "respectful" to him. This was a man who called every woman in the office either "honey" or "baby"! He replaced me with a man, but more frustratingly, he dismissed my emotional and professional response to this replacement by saying "why do you want a career anyway, wouldn't you rather have kids before it's too late?" Once I reached the level of holding a leadership role, I found that several of my male colleagues struggled to remember my name, confusing me with other women in their teams, often my juniors, whilst never having the same issue amongst the men in the room. Many meetings started with a comment on my appearance - both positive or negative! - whilst the men never seemed subject to this scrutiny or feedback. At major presentations when I performed well and I knew I had outperformed my male peers, my appearance was credited. "I really like the way you flicked your hair". There was no mention of the content of my presentation or my delivery of the content. Again, none of this did I classify in my head as discrimination. It was just "how things are". The fact that I did well and progressed made me push it back in my mind and ignore the bigger picture.

Also choosing not to have children - an active choice of mine and my husband's - is something that made me feel like I really couldn't comment or complain even when it crossed my mind in later years. The act of not having children is still one that gets judged intensely - and more often by other women than men. The level of explanation people feel is due to them is sometimes astonishing! It's only in the recent times that I internalised this as discrimination or bias, and I realised how I needed to make sure that I made a positive change in any way that I could to build the leaders of our future.

Here is how you can be an active ally to someone like me...

I wish I had had an ally when I was younger when I didn't see these incidents as incidents of bias and discrimination myself. It might not always have solved things but someone saying "that wasn't ok" and making it clear that I should expect more from my colleagues, leaders and company, would have been incredibly valuable. You get desensitised over time - partly as a coping mechanism so having that clarity and insight would have been hugely helpful, and probably still is.

I would also appreciate having someone to talk through how to deal with situations where you feel bias or discrimination. I know that bias and discrimination can come from anyone - including some of your closest supporters, colleagues and friends. Knowing how to tackle it is hard and having a safe space to talk through different options, recognising that every situation is going to be different would be hugely helpful.

At times I would want an ally to point out the issue, not to me but to the others in the room. I am extremely used to being "the only woman in the room" but that also comes with exhaustion sometimes at not wanting to be constantly saying the same things or pointing out the same microaggressions. Someone being willing to step in, to take the pressure off me to constantly raise it would be invaluable.

Daniel Newton (He/Him)

I am a stay-at-home dad to our two young children. Until recently, I was a solicitor in an international law firm headquartered in London. My wife and I wanted one of us to take on the role of being the primary caregiver once our children reached an age where they needed more than the basics of food and love (our eldest daughter is 5). Once we assessed who would be best in which role, we settled on me stopping work completely and my wife continuing to work full time. My wife loves looking after the children and I really enjoyed my job, so we had the luxury of choosing between a range of good options in order to find something that worked best for us and our children.

My story here is based on the following intersectional dimensions of diversity: Gender - Marital & parenthood choices

Here is my story of bias and discrimination...

I am generally a beneficiary of people's biases. I am after all a tall, white, heterosexual male, and whilst I have made a choice that is unusual, it hasn't seemed to change the privileges I enjoy so I have faced relatively few examples of bias affecting me negatively. More commonly, the reaction to my decision to resign from a high paying and prestigious job to look after our children has been met with either envy or confusion. I have had some people assume that I've been made redundant and that I'm pretending it was my decision to resign but they seem to be a minority. Usually, I receive congratulations for being brave and kind words of encouragement.

I expect my wife is likely to face more negative reactions from our decision. She may be seen to have abandoned her duties as a mother in favour of her career. Whilst this view is incorrect, and wouldn't be held against a man who was a sole breadwinner, I expect it is something she will have to face in the years to come. On top of that, she will have to miss all sorts of moments I'll be having with the children whilst she is working. I really feel that I've got the better side of the deal - but so does she, which is why I think our arrangement will work out just fine in the end.

Here is how you can be an active ally to someone like me...

Start with questioning your own assumptions and stereotypes about parenthood. When my decision has been met by confusion, generally the easiest way to help people understand the decision is to point out that for a long-time women have been leaving jobs like mine in order to look after their children and their husbands have carried on as sole breadwinner. Obvious though it sounds, it is often not a parallel that the person has drawn for themselves and when they see it, they at least begin to understand how the arrangement may work. For some of them, their own wife was the one who left a high-profile career. Bizarrely, considering how bright these people are, the gender difference seems to block their ability to see the parallels!

My allies are other primary caregivers - predominately mothers, nannies and childminders. I just need them to be friendly, be inclusive and not leave me on my own just because I'm a man!

4
EMPATHETIC ENGAGEMENT

*"Learning to stand in somebody else's shoes,
to see through their eyes, that's how peace begins.
And it's up to you to make that happen."*

BARACK OBAMA, *the first African-American
president of the United States*

Have you ever become more aware of something and then you seem to see it everywhere? It could be a new word, a particular song, a new model of a car…or even biases. As we reflect and gain a better understanding of the biases that exist around us, we not only become more aware of our own biases but we might also begin to notice biases everywhere. This is not because there has necessarily been an increase in the occurrences of biases; they have always been there, but rather because of the phenomenon known as the Baader-Meinhof phenomenon or more commonly, frequency illusion or recency bias.

Frequency illusion or *recency bias* is a cognitive bias. *Cognitive biases* are systematic errors in thinking. These occur when people process and interpret information in the world around them resulting in decisions and judgments that deviate from the norm and/or rationality. The frequency illusion or recency bias describes our tendency to see new information, names, ideas or patterns everywhere soon after they first come to our attention. As our awareness increases, we assume that it is actually happening more frequently or in greater numbers when, in fact, this may not be the case. This phenomenon was first described in 1994 by a reader of a newspaper in the state of Minnesota in the United States. Having just heard about the ultra-leftwing Baader-Meinhof terrorist group in former West Germany, the reader saw the name Baader-Meinhof everywhere.

Our brain has an incredible ability for pattern recognition. It's the way our brain prevents itself from getting cognitively overwhelmed with the vast amount of information coming its way. To process this vast amount of information, our brain uses two cognitive processes: selective attention and confirmation bias. For example, when reading a novel, our brain is unable to process, retain and remember everything we are reading. Instead, our brain uses selective attention to remember the parts of the novel that interest us or the parts we make connections with based on our own life experiences. Our brain then goes one step further to seek information in the novel to confirm that those connections are indeed the ones that are important or relevant for us to know. What is known as confirmation bias.

So if you feel that you are suddenly seeing biases and discrimination everywhere; this might be the reason why. Yet these biases and acts of discrimination have always been there, in various forms and at varying levels of intensity throughout human history. It can, however, feel uncomfortable to suddenly become so overtly aware of them. If you are feeling this way, I want to assure you that it is a natural and reasonable response, and an essential one to active allyship. The question is - what can we do about these biases that we seem to see everywhere?

Here comes empathetic engagement.

No one likes their biases being pointed out. Not me, and no one I know. When others make us aware of our biases, our defence mechanisms kick in. We feel that we are being "attacked" in an unfair way.

Our responses can range from anger to embarrassment. We may even verbally respond, saying "Come on, I didn't mean it that way!" or "That was just a passing comment, don't take things so seriously," or "Where's your sense of humour, it was just a joke!" Most of us consider ourselves to be "good people" (which we are), but we have a false belief that good people are not biased. Except, *everyone* has biases.

Therefore, addressing biases needs to be done in a way that does not create fear; that does not trigger the walls of defence into going up; that prevents people from feeling like they are walking on eggshells or are under the microscope all the time. We need to engage with each other to address biases in a way that focuses on empathy.

Empathy is the ability to vicariously understand and share the feelings and experiences of others. When we engage empathetically, we make efforts to try and see things from another perspective, we try to imagine ourselves in someone else's situation. How can we draw on empathy to engage in a way that helps us all become more aware of our biases, with the aim of making our workplaces more inclusive for all?

Beware and be aware of "termite biases"

Before we get deeper into what empathetic engagement entails, I want to explore the idea of *termite biases*. If the very thought of termites crawling around makes you squirm, you aren't alone. While you may not have heard the term termite biases, you may be more familiar with the term 'microaggression'. Coined by Dr. Chester Pierce in the 1970s in his work with African Americans, microaggressions are statements, actions, or incidents that are considered to be an instance of indirect, subtle, or unintentional discrimination against members of a marginalised group. However, it was only in 2007 that the term resurfaced thanks to psychologist Derald Wing Sue. Here is the thing, we assume that overt biases cause significant harm to those being discriminated against. They do. However, research also shows us that subtle biases and discrimination have an equally negative impact on our psychological and physical health, as well as work-related behaviour.[59]

So while we recognise this, the term 'microaggressions' gives the impression that these biases are small and perhaps less impactful. According to Ruchika Tulshyan, the author of the book *Inclusion on Purpose: An Intersectional Approach to Creating a Culture of Belonging at Work,* "The term 'microaggression' doesn't fully capture the actions' emotional and material effects or how they impact women and people of color's career progressions."[60] In Ruchika's *HBR* article "We Need to Retire the Term 'Microaggressions'", Ruchika draws on the work of Derald Wing Sue: "Daily microaggressions 'create a lowered sense of psychological well-being. They deplete psychic energy or problem-solving and work productivity.' Why? Microaggressions are cumulative. 'They occur to people of color from the time they awaken, until they go to bed, from the time they are born until they die.'"[61]

These 'micro' behaviours are much like a quiet disease, silently eating away at inclusion. While I myself use the term microaggressions because it is a well-recognised term in the DEI field, I prefer to refer to these kinds of indirect, subtle and unintentional biases as *termite biases*. Why? Because termites do more damage to our economy than any other pest, but crucially, you don't even know they are there until significant damage has been done. Much like these biases. While we are more aware and have greater understanding about the biases that manifest themselves as overt and obvious aggressions, we are less aware and have limited understanding about the many times when our unconscious biases express themselves as *termite biases*.

Termite biases are often expressed unintentionally by people who may be well-intentioned. They can be mistaken for a casual comment, be brushed aside as humour or even sound like a compliment. They may go unnoticed by others and even by the receiver. Termite biases are communicated through subtle language and may be indirectly communicated, making it difficult to know if you are committing one. If they sound relatively harmless, they aren't. Termite biases - when experienced repeatedly and frequently - make people feel undervalued, unappreciated, and generally offended - unincluded. After all, it's often the little things that sting the most.

Termite biases

Brief, subtle and indirect biases that unintentionally or intentionally communicate stereotypes, prejudices, derogatory or negative attitudes towards others, and are often mistaken for a casual comment, humour or a compliment. When experienced repeatedly and frequently, they make people feel undervalued, unappreciated, and unincluded.

Termite biases take many forms. Here are some examples of termite biases with explanations of why they are actually biases. As these biases may not be obvious, they can be challenging to spot:

• Saying to a woman who has been recently hired into a managerial/leadership role: "Congrats on your new role. You are so fortunate to be a woman, there are so many opportunities for you." assuming that the only reason she was hired was because of her gender-identity, not because she was actually qualified for the role.

- Assuming that a new female colleague who "looks young" is an intern based on the assumption that seniority of age is a prerequisite for seniority in hierarchy.

- Pressing someone to answer, "Where are you actually from?" based on assumptions that someone who looks like them can't actually be from the place they say they are from.

- Asking someone wearing workwear from their culture (for example, the Dashiki from West Africa or a Saree from India) or religious clothing such as a hijab, turban or bindi: "Is that really what you would wear to work in your home country? Doesn't seem very professional." based on a cookie cutter definition of what professional work wear looks like, usually based on Western societies.

- Commenting to someone with kinky or curly hair: "Wow, your hair is so big today. Are you planning on coming like that for our client meeting?" based on the assumption of what professional hair looks like, usually straight hair.

- Commenting to someone for whom English is their first language that "you speak English so well!" based on the assumption that someone who looks like them should not be able to speak English so well.

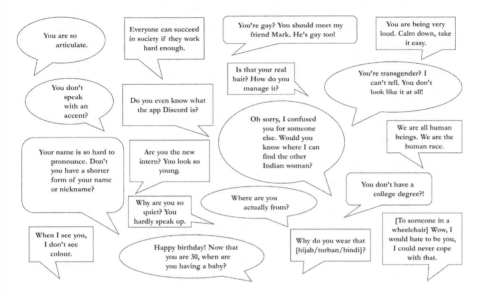

Examples of termite biases

When termite biases are pointed out, they are often dismissed by the person who is being held accountable for them. "I was actually complimenting you." "Oh come on, I was just joking." "You're just being over-sensitive; it was just a casual comment." Very often, fearing these responses, those on the receiving end of a termite bias may not bring it up. They may even rationalise the bias as being a one-off incident and tell themselves: "I'm sure they didn't mean it that way" or "I'm sure I'm overthinking this" or "I'm sure they were just joking."

We have all been at lunch or in a meeting where someone makes an inappropriate joke and others force a fake laugh. The room gets an uncomfortable vibe and people wriggle in their seats - you get the picture, right? The discomfort is usually only broken when someone changes the subject, because quite often we don't know how to react in such a situation, or we don't want to be labelled as the "woke police" with no sense of humour.

Workplaces are not comedy studios - and we are not stand-up comedians. Yes, we need to have an environment of collegiality, but humour at the expense of others should not be accepted in workplace cultures that promote inclusion - or anywhere for that matter. There should be zero tolerance in today's organisations for jokes that are sexist, racist, ableist, homophobic or transphobic in nature. If humour at the expense of others has been part of organisational life, it is only because we have been socially conditioned to accept it and have not known how to address it. There must be more to joke about than other people, right? Even self-deprecating humour or self-irony can be tricky - when done about yourself and only yourself, that's your choice and absolutely acceptable. However, when it also stereotypes others of a group that you are a part of, it can reaffirm and propagate those very stereotypes and their associated biases. Jokes about invisible dimensions of diversity like sexual orientation, marital situations, neurodiversity, and socio-economic backgrounds are particularly toxic because the target of the joke could be in the room without the person sharing the joke even knowing it - and that results in people hiding their identities, preventing people from bringing their whole diverse selves to work.

What about compliments? How can something meant to be nice be harmful? When compliments are based on assumptions and expectations about someone, then they have the potential to reflect the underlying biases. Let me share a few examples: "Wow, you're so articulate!", "You speak good English" or "You don't speak with an accent". All of these comments assume that the person is expected to have poor English language competencies, expected to have an accent from the region of the world they are presumed to be from based on their physical appearances, or expected to be inarticulate. This happens to many people of colour from non-English speaking countries. Another example is when Asian students from China, Korea, India and other parts of Asia get asked for help with a maths or science question; based on a stereotype about a particular ethnic group being good at something.

What about the things that seem to be coming from a place of good intention like "Everyone can succeed if they work hard enough" or "When I see you, I don't see colour" or "There is only one race, the human race"? Statements like these do not recognise that the world is experienced very differently by different people. Our natural desire to assume that life is experienced the same way and our deep discomfort with accepting that it isn't is often at the root of these statements, comments like: "I can't be homophobic, I have gay friends" or "I can't be racist, I have friends who are people of colour". Having friends who are from under-represented, marginalised and discriminated groups is lovely - and should quite frankly be natural and not something to be celebrated as something special - but does not mean we don't hold biases about those groups. What about this one: "I believe that we should hire the person who is the best fit for the job and our company"? I have noticed that many organisations use this as an excuse to continue hiring to fit the cookie cutter, propagating the bias that someone who doesn't fit the mould is not a competent hire.

Termite biases are not always expressed through what is often passed off as humour or as a compliment. They can also be expressed in other ways. For example, a White person clutching their bag tighter as a Black person passes by, the owner of a store following a person of colour around or when a White person waits to take the next elevator when a Black or Brown person is on it. All of these are based on the assumption that the person of colour is more likely to be dangerous, a threat or even a criminal. During a recent workplace event I was mistaken for the only other Indian woman in that context. The person's response? "Oh sorry,

I got the wrong person". Mixing up people from under-represented groups reflects the assumption that people from an under-represented group "look the same". I felt unseen and the incident influenced my feeling of belonging in that context. I know of Black and Brown men who were mistaken for taxi drivers or food delivery drivers in the workplace lobby or reception area. In 2020, British Vogue editor Edward Enninful, one of few Black editors in the publishing industry in the UK, was told to enter via the loading bay by a third-party security guard as he reached his office.[62] I also know of men of colour who are treated differently at high-end car showrooms, assumed to be unable to afford to buy a car. On one occasion, a Brown friend of mine was directed towards the taxi dealership section of a luxury car manufacturer!

There are also termite biases embedded in the casual comments or phrases that are frequently used. These usually make reference to a particular ethnic group or to a form of disability in a casual way. They can also take the form of nicknames reflecting biases about certain groups.

- "I am a slave to my work." The use of the word 'slave' can trigger feelings of non-inclusion and discrimination with certain ethnic communities that have had a history of being oppressed due to slavery and colonialism.
- "These are Chinese whispers" or "It's all Greek to me" or "He's speaking double Dutch." These phrases link ethnic groups with negative stereotypes.
- "This is lame/dumb" or "Mute yourself" (this phrase was commonly used on Teams or Zoom calls through the COVID pandemic) or "blind recruitment"/ "that's my blind spot" or "this is our team's handicap." These phrases perpetuate the perception that having a disability is a negative thing.

- "Alright Gramps/Grandma", "Ok Boomer", "Snowflakes", "Borat" (derogatory term for Eastern Europeans based on the movie character) or "Gora/Gori" (derogatory term in the Hindi language against White men/women) or "Ching Chong/Chink/Chinky" (derogatory term mocking a person of Chinese descent) or "Banana/Coconut/ Oreo" (derogatory term referring to someone Chinese/Indian/ Black who is perceived as trying to be White). These nicknames all reflect ageism and racial biases.

In the workplace, termite biases can take the form of the following behaviours:

- *Domrupting*: Occurs when a member of a dominant group unnecessarily cuts off someone from an under-represented group during a meeting or group discussion session. This term was inspired by the concept of manterrupting. Did you know that women are interrupted far more frequently than men during meetings and panel discussions? 33% more frequently.[63]
- *Dompropriating*: Occurs when a member of a dominant group takes credit for an idea shared by someone from an under-represented group. This term was inspired by the colloquial term bropropriating for instances when a man takes credit for a woman's idea.
- *Domsplaining*: Occurs when a member of a dominant group explains something to someone from an under-represented group in a condescending or patronising tone, based on the assumption that the person from the under-represented group does not have the capability and knowledge about the issue at hand, or is emotional and lacking rational thinking abilities. This term is based on the term mansplaining which was made famous in 2008 by author Rebecca Solnit's famous essay, "Men Explain Things to Me".

While we have made some progress in becoming more aware and intentional in the language we use and in our behaviours when it comes to more obvious biases, we are sometimes oblivious to the termite biases embedded in the words we use and actions we take ourselves and of those around us. These termite biases are the silent enemy when it comes to nurturing inclusive workplaces for all. If we do not address these, we do not stand a chance at progressing towards more diverse and inclusive environments.

So how can you be an active ally to prevent a termite bias infestation from taking place in your team and organisation? How can you be an active ally to your colleagues when they experience bias, and even to yourself when you experience bias?

Empathetic engagement at work

When we witness or experience a bias, particularly termite biases, we have three options as an active ally:

- We can choose to do nothing.
- We can choose to address it at that moment.
- We can choose to address it at a later time.

While there are some situations when addressing biases can get you arrested or put you in physical danger, making it perfectly reasonable to not address a bias - such as participating in a Pride parade in a country where homosexuality is illegal - we have done nothing for far too long. We need to act. At the same time, when you are the one experiencing bias, addressing it can be emotionally exhausting. You may even feel that addressing biases may have a negative impact on your career. These are all real considerations to weigh. There are consequences both in addressing bias and in not addressing it.

Take a moment to reflect. Have you witnessed a colleague experience a termite bias during a meeting or at lunch? Or have you had a colleague come to you distressed about a bias they experienced? What did you say to them? Did you try to help them forget about it, or diminish their experience, telling them they might be too sensitive?

Unfortunately, these brush-asides (also known as gaslighting) by those of us who could be active allies serve only to discount feelings of discrimination and support the continued perpetuation of such termite biases.

One thing is clear, we need to do more to address biases when we witness or experience them. Being a bystander is not an option if we want inclusive workplaces for all. So what can you do beyond saying "I am sorry this happened to you"?

Steps for empathetic engagement

We have a choice about when we address a bias that you have witnessed or experienced: at the time it occurred or at a later time. Deciding which is dependent on the relationship that the people involved have with each other, how safe they feel with each other in addressing biases, and the cultural sensitivities associated with addressing an issue in front of others. You are the best person to sense the room or context and decide whether you would like to address the bias at the moment or at a later time, perhaps in a one-to-one meeting or a smaller setting with someone from HR depending on the severity of the bias in question. If you are speaking up for someone else at the time the bias occurred, be sure to not jump in as the saviour when the person is not looking for one and rob the person of their agency to address the bias themselves. If you are planning on addressing the bias at a later time, you could consider checking with the person impacted by the bias to make sure they are comfortable with you doing so. Read their reaction and the vibe in the room to decide what you should do. This takes time to get the hang of, and we are all likely to make mistakes along the way. The most important thing for us to remember is that we are aiming for progress, not perfection.

The steps laid out below are primarily to help you address termite biases as an active ally. When there are blatant, more serious or obvious sexist, racist, homophobic or transphobic biases at play, what may be needed is to *call out* the bias at the moment. This may mean saying something like: "That's not okay, I need to stop you there" or "What you said is not in line with our company's values, please stop there" or "That word is really offensive, find another one" or even "Have you considered the impact of what you just said?". When there are serious cases of sexism or racism or homophobia or transphobia, always reach out to your HR business partner to align on the best course of action.

Addressing it at the time: Power of empathetic questions and comments

No one likes to be confronted, and the human reaction to confrontation is to become defensive. Given this, termite biases need to be addressed in a non-confrontational way - our tone matters. Asking questions or making comments in the right tone can be a powerful tool for getting those around us to have an "aha" moment, one in which they discover a bias they weren't aware of.

These questions/comments could include:

→ Why don't you tell me more about your choice of words here?

→ How did you get to that decision/conclusion?

→ How do you know it is working? What evidence would you have to demonstrate that?

→ I didn't understand the joke, would you be able to please explain it to me?

→ Have you looked at other options? What were they and why was this the best way forward?

→ Why do you think that?

→ What was your intention in saying that? Do you think your intention may have been different from the impact of your words?

→ I'm curious. What did you mean by that?

→ What led you to draw that conclusion?

→ That's an interesting way of looking at it, why don't you tell me more?

→ Can you help me understand why you reacted that way?

→ To address domrupting: Hang on, I don't believe Imani was finished sharing their thoughts.

→ To address dompropriating: Thank you for paraphrasing Valentina's idea, that is indeed a very refreshing idea, X.

→ To address domsplaining: Hang on, I'm sure Li understands this well and does not need an explanation.

Addressing it at a later time: Engaging in an empathetic dialogue

If you choose to address it at a later time, don't wait too long after the bias occurs. You don't want to be in a situation where the relevant parties have forgotten the context in which the bias happened. Involve HR depending on the severity of the situation, or if you need support. This may be especially helpful when there is a power imbalance between yourself and the other person, like when the person who is being biased is your manager or your CEO.

Step 1: Invite the person who engaged in the bias to a meeting. You may choose to involve HR. Book a meeting room so the atmosphere feels safer than being out in the open. Start by saying something along the lines of:

"I would like to speak to you about something on my mind. I understand that this can be uncomfortable, but I would appreciate it if you let me finish what I have to say before we discuss it."

Step 2: Explain clearly what was said or done. Details always help so the person can't deny it.

"In the meeting the other day, you said/did …".

Step 3: Explain how it made you/someone else feel. Allow enough room in your explanation to give the person space to respond later.

"When you said/did _____, it seems like you are _____, but I am not sure if this is what you mean. However, what you said/did made me/ the other person feel … I would like you to imagine how it must have felt for me/the other person."

If the person gets defensive, politely ask them to wait until you are finished.

"I understand that you may have said/done this unintentionally, but I would really like you to let me finish."

If they continue to get defensive, you may wish to ask them to not dismiss your/the other person's experience.

"I understand this is hard for you, but please do not dismiss this life experience of mine/theirs. It has had an impact and I would like to engage in a constructive dialogue about this once I finish sharing my side. After all, we all have biases, right?"

Step 4: Offer suggestions for what the person can do differently. Suggest what they can say or do to communicate their point in a way that does not perpetuate a bias or highlight that the bias is inappropriate and should not be repeated. Use credible data or research to support why you have brought this up.

"Research/Data shows us that…In the future, it would be better if you …"

Step 5: Give the other person time to reflect and respond.

"I know this is a lot to process, would you like to take a moment and then we can discuss this? I would like us to find a way forward."

Now, what if it is *your* biases that are being pointed out; you are at the receiving end of the above, how should you respond? Here are some tips:

→ Listen intently. Don't interrupt. Ask for clarifications only when needed or after the person has finished saying what they wanted to.

→ Don't get defensive or dismiss the person's concerns. We have to understand this harsh truth - in addressing termite biases, it is not about you; it is about the impact of what you said/did on the other person, the receiver of the bias. So don't get defensive - don't say that you didn't mean it or that it was unintentional or that you are coming from "a place of good intention". Don't justify your words or actions by saying things like "I didn't mean it, it was just a casual comment" or "it was just a joke" or "you're being over-sensitive, it's not a big deal. Lighten up".

→ Once the person finishes what they wanted to say, acknowledge that you recognise that it has had a negative impact. Apologise but don't over-apologise. Overdoing an apology can make it uncomfortable for the other person, and even make the other person feel bad for bringing the bias up. Active allies show empathy, and even emotions, when openly speaking about uncomfortable issues.[64]

"I am sorry that what I said/did made you feel that way."

→ Respond in a way that shows that you are willing to reflect and take their feedback into account.

"Thank you for bringing this to my attention. I will try to do better."

"Good catch, thanks for noticing it."x

→ Take time afterwards to introspect honestly and deeply. Reflect on how what you said or did had an effect of non-inclusion on the other person. That is where empathy comes in. Ask yourself:

How was what I said or did received by the other person?

What impact did it have on them?

What can I do to make sure I don't do this again to the same person or someone else?

Addressing biases is not easy. Believe me, I know. There are times when I am in a frame of mind to ask the right questions or bring up the bias in a way that prevents the walls of defence from going up. In those situations, I feel content that I have been an active ally and been able to engage in a meaningful conversation with the other person. There are, however, other times when I get it wrong. I may start off well by asking an empathetic question but the response (usually one that is dismissive) is hurtful or triggering, and then it is much harder to stick to the script to engage empathetically. What I have found is that the more comfortable I get with engaging in empathetic conversations, the easier it becomes for me to more consistently respond in empathetic ways when I witness or experience bias. So while it is not easy, it is a new "muscle" to build, and just like any other muscle, in order to make it stronger, we need to build up strength over time. I am working on empathetic engagement, are you?

Empathetic engagement means:
- Having an awareness of the existence of termite biases.
- Being able to recognise and identify termite biases and what they look and sound like.
- Not getting defensive or dismissing the experience of bias.
- Knowing what to say/do when you witness or experience bias.
- Knowing how to respond when your biases are pointed out.

Putting yourself in someone else's shoes

Let us try and imagine how the world is experienced by someone whose identity is very different from our own.

1. Pick an identity from the list below. Some of these identities describe single dimensions of diversity while others have multiple dimensions that make up a person's intersectional identity. Pick an identity that is different from your own. The identities are intentionally brief. You can of course repeat this exercise with each of the identities below.

- ☐ An ethnically African woman
- ☐ An ethnically South Asian man
- ☐ A 25-year-old man with an ethnic last name
- ☐ A man wearing a turban
- ☐ An autistic man
- ☐ A Black man
- ☐ A White man business leader
- ☐ A White woman business leader
- ☐ A transgender individual
- ☐ A person in a wheelchair
- ☐ A person identifying as non-binary
- ☐ A refugee
- ☐ A woman wearing a hijab for religious reasons

☐ An introvert

☐ An Indigenous woman

☐ A White man who is an ex-convict

☐ A single mother and woman of colour

☐ A pregnant woman of colour

☐ An LGBTQ+ person of colour

☐ A person of colour in a wheelchair

☐ An autistic person of colour

☐ A gay father and person of colour

☐ A White, gay, visually impaired man

☐ A Muslim man

☐ A 63-year-old man

2. Imagine that for the next few minutes, you are the person whose identity you have chosen above. You can assume you are in your country/city/organisation. No other contextual information is provided; you should make any assumptions needed and make efforts to make a mental note of what these assumptions were.

3. Below are seven statements. Mark where you lie in the level of your agreement to each statement. You should 'listen' to your immediate response, not including ethical/moral considerations. There may be situations where you may partially agree and please make a note of that. Do not discuss your character or your responses with anyone else.

This person is likely to feel part of the 'team' at work.

Agree .... Disagree

This person would be listened to in most situations.

Agree .... Disagree

This person is likely to have a good education.

Agree .... Disagree

This person is likely to have high career ambitions.

Agree .... Disagree

This person is likely to feel comfortable speaking up at a business meeting.

Agree .... Disagree

This person is likely to be invited for a job interview.

Agree .... Disagree

This person is likely to feel safe walking down the street at night.

Agree .... Disagree

4. Reflect on the following questions:

What are your first reactions or thoughts? How did you feel during the activity?

....
....
....
....
....

Who were you thinking of? Describe the person below. Was the person based on someone you know?

....
....
....
....
....
....

What assumptions were you making about this person to help you answer the question?

....
....
....
....
....

Did you feel uncomfortable/unsure about how someone like the character would react/ respond? Did you feel you didn't know much about this person? How many times did you think "I just don't know?" or "It depends on the person or the situation."

....
....
....
....
....
....

What surprised you the most?

....
....
....
....
....
....

What are you taking away with you today from this exercise?

....
....
....
....
....
....

Optional: Do this activity as a team or group activity

As the facilitator of this exercise, it is important to create an environment of non-judgement for this exercise, and that begins with the facilitator. Your tone and mannerisms matter.

Prior to the session:

1. Each person in the group needs to be assigned an identity from the list below. The identities below can be printed on pieces of paper to be handed out to participants at random. They can also be individually emailed to participants as well.

   - An ethnically African woman
   - An ethnically South Asian man
   - A 25-year-old man with an ethnic last name
   - A man wearing a turban
   - An autistic man
   - A Black man
   - A White man business leader
   - A White woman business leader
   - A transgender individual
   - A person in a wheelchair
   - A person identifying as non-binary
   - A refugee
   - A woman wearing a hijab for religious reasons
   - An introvert
   - An Indigenous woman
   - A White man who is an ex-convict

- A single mother and woman of colour
- A pregnant woman of colour
- An LGBTQ+ person of colour
- A person of colour in a wheelchair
- An autistic person of colour
- A gay father and person of colour
- A White, gay, visually impaired man
- A Muslim man
- A 63-year-old man

2. Read through how to conduct this activity. Familiarise yourself well with the activity.

At the session:

1. Read out the following instructions to the participants:

- Imagine that for the next few minutes, you are the person whose identity you have been given. You should not share your identity with anyone else until you are told to do so. You should not discuss your character with anyone else.
- You may assume that you are in [insert your company name].
- No other contextual information will be given; you should make any assumptions needed and make efforts to remember what these assumptions were.
- Seven statements will be read to you, one at a time. If you agree with the statement, step forward. If you do not agree, stay where you are. There may be situations where you may partially agree, and you may take a smaller step forward accordingly.

- There should be no discussion or consulting each other in between the statements.
- At the end, you should not share your character until told to do so.

2. Begin with the statements, reading one at a time and asking participants to step forward if they agree.

Statement 1: This person is likely to feel part of the 'team' at work.
Statement 2: This person would be listened to in most situations.
Statement 3: This person is likely to have a good education.
Statement 4: This person is likely to have high career ambitions.
Statement 5: This person is likely to feel comfortable speaking up at a business meeting.
Statement 6: This person is likely to be invited for a job interview.
Statement 7: This person is likely to feel safe walking down the street at night.

3. Debrief:

Before asking the participants to reveal their characters, ask each of them to share one word/ short phrase to describe their initial thoughts. Then ask each person to share the identity given to them and ask an additional probing question (see below) to individual participants or open to the group depending on the time available. Ensure that everyone gets a chance to share their thoughts and reflections.

- How did you feel during the activity?
- To which statements did you raise your hand/when did you hesitate/when were you clear that you disagreed with the statement?
- What surprised you the most?
- What assumptions did you make?
- How many of you felt uncomfortable/unsure about how someone like the character would react/respond?
- What are you taking away with you today from this activity?

Empathetic engagement: practice makes progress

When we are confronted with bias - either experiencing it ourselves or witnessing it - we are often at a loss of words. We sometimes muster up an uncomfortable laugh, expression or response, hoping that the discomfort in the room will go away. We may quickly change the topic of conversation to ease the discomfort. We might not address the bias because we don't know how to and we fear the walls of defence that are likely to come up, so simply saying "that was biased" is not an ideal option.

With the steps of empathetic engagement laid out in this chapter, hopefully you feel better equipped to address biases. Practice always makes progress. The first few times will be hard but the more comfortable we get at using questions and comments to engage empathetically on biases, the easier it becomes.

So let's get practising. Pick any of the termite biases below. Imagine that this bias has been said to you or that you have witnessed it being said to someone else. How would you respond? You can use the guide below to help you along.

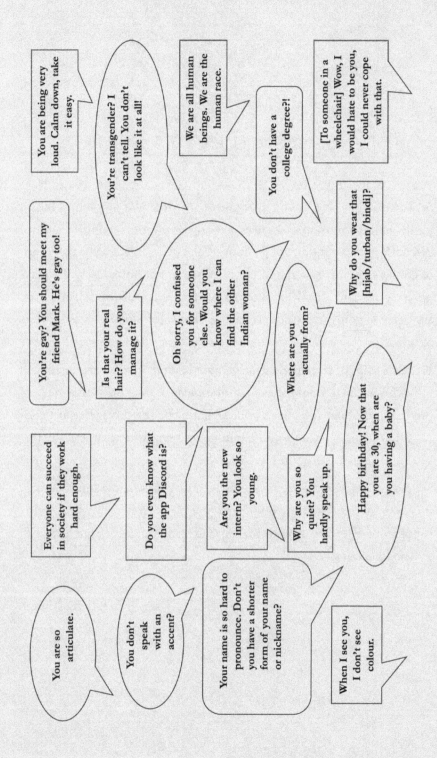

Which termite bias have you chosen?

....

....

....

....

Have you
- ☐ Experienced it yourself?
- ☐ Witnessed it being communicated to someone else?
- ☐ Would you address the bias
- ☐ At the time it was communicated?
- ☐ At a later time?

If you are addressing the bias at the time it was communicated, which question(s)/comment(s) would you use?

- ☐ Why don't you tell me more (about your choice of words)?
- ☐ How did you get to that decision?
- ☐ I didn't understand the joke, would you be able to please explain it to me?
- ☐ Have you looked at other options? What were they and why was this the best way forward?
- ☐ Why do you think that?
- ☐ What did you mean by that?
- ☐ What led you to draw that conclusion?
- ☐ That's an interesting way of looking at it, why did you say that?
- ☐ Can you help me understand why you reacted that way?

If you are addressing the bias at a later time, practice the following steps. You can of course choose your own sentences that reflect your own style of communication. The suggestions here are only to guide you along the journey.

Step 1: Invite the person who engaged in the bias to a meeting. How would you start the conversation?

"I would like to speak to you about something on my mind. I understand that this can be uncomfortable, but I would appreciate it if you let me finish what I have to say before we discuss it."

....
....
....
....
....
....
....
....
....
....
....
....
....
....
....

Step 2: Explain clearly what was said or done. Details always help so the person can't deny it.

"In the meeting the other day, you said/did …".

....

....

....

....

....

....

....

....

Step 3: Explain how it made you/someone else feel. Allow enough room in your explanation to give the person space to respond later.

"When you said/did _____, it seems like you are _____, but I am not sure if this is what you mean. However, what you said/did made me/ the other person feel … I would like you to imagine how it must have felt for me/the other person."

....

....

....

....

....

....

....

Imagine that the person gets defensive, how would you respond?

"I understand that you may have said/done this unintentionally, but I would really like you to let me finish."

"I understand this is hard for you, but please do not dismiss this life experience of mine/theirs. It has had an impact and I would like to engage in a constructive dialogue about this once I finish sharing my side. After all, we all have biases, right?"

....

....

....

....

....

....

Step 4: Offer suggestions for what the person can do differently. Use credible data or research to support why you have brought this up.

"Research/Data shows us that…In the future, it would be better if you …"

....

....

....

....

....

....

....

Step 5: Give the other person time to reflect and respond.

"I know this is a lot to process, would you like to take a moment and then we can discuss this. I would like us to find a way forward."

....

....

....

....

....

....

....

Now imagine that it is your biases being pointed out. How would you respond if you are the one receiving this feedback about your own biases? Below are some tips. Which ones would you like to practice more of?

- ☐ Listening more intently and limiting interruptions.
- ☐ Not getting defensive or dismissing the person's concerns.
- ☐ Acknowledging that you recognise that it has had a negative impact; apologising without over-apologising.
- ☐ Responding in a way that shows that you are willing to reflect and take their feedback into account: *"Good catch, thanks for noticing it. I will try to do better"*
- ☐ Taking time to introspect honestly and deeply.

Repeat these steps with the other termite biases or biases we have looked at so far in this chapter.

Chris Hovde (He/Him)

I'm a gay urban monk who is passionate about my purpose to make people and robots fight together for a better society. My core values are regenerativity, equality and authenticity.

I have years of experience from various leadership positions and HR in large international companies such as Telia, IKEA and the Varner Group. I have also been the CEO of an Oslo-based healthcare clinic called Balder. I have been nominated for a number of awards for my work within digitalization, leadership and diversity and inclusion.

I'm currently working as the Global People Movement Lead at Telia Company, Chairman of the Board of Future Leaders Global, Made to Grow, Hagegata 31 and am the Founder of Regenerative Monks. I live in a jungle in the poorest part of Oslo, the capital of Norway, with my little French bulldog, Buddha.

My story here is based on the following intersectional dimensions of diversity: Sexual orientation - Educational background - Personality - Neurodiversity - Beliefs and practices (lifestyle choices)

Here is my story of bias and discrimination...

I was bullied a lot when I was young because I only had female friends; I could relate more to them because of their empathy and maturity. I have also always related more to older people than younger people. Moving a lot didn't make it any easier to establish roots and grow confident in my own identity.

At a bar, I was once beaten to the ground by a straight man, because he felt that by looking at him, I was a threat since I'm gay. He asked me, "what are you looking at?" And then beat my head against the handrail so hard that I got a severe concussion and needed to stay home from work for 2 weeks to recover.

In an interview round for a managerial position, I was advised by the recruiter to talk about my partner as 'she' instead of 'he' so that I would be more likely to get the job. I refused to go further with that process. A few days ago, at the lunch table at work, a group of straight men were chatting loudly. When a colleague said he was going to the Greek island Mykonos, one person questioned why he was going to that faggot (offensive term referring to someone who is gay) island? "Isn't that only for faggots?".

On a professional front and as someone who works within HR, I have faced many biases. Once a man spilled some coffee on the floor on purpose and said that I should clean it up, adding: "Isn't that why HR is here?" When it comes to my educational background, most of my career has been in leadership roles. When I joined HR, I felt almost bullied because of my lack of formal education within the HR profession. A manager even escalated it to my manager and said that they were questioning my HR competence. When I found this out, I went up to the manager and said: "You don't need to question my formal HR education, because I have none! But I have 14 years of management experience, and I guess that's a better support for you than a bachelor in HR."

When it comes to my personality I have always been referred to as being "too engaged", "too loud", "too different". In fact, I find being gay the easiest aspect of being different. I dress differently. I have a different attitude to life being an extreme minimalist and being eco-friendly. I live a life without drinking alcohol, and focusing on nature, meditation, and on the greater good. I find that justifying these lifestyle choices of mine is so much harder than being gay.

Here is how you can be an active ally to someone like me…

Let's agree to never agree. We are different people and will live different lives in so many ways. Let's instead be curious about each other, show respect and love. My reality will never be yours, but we can make an effort to learn and understand more about each other. Where nobody fits in is where everybody fits in. Because we don't need to try to fit in, we just need to be more of our own brilliant authentic selves. That's a world that I dream of.

Vivienne Robinson (She/Her)

I am a wife to a frequently travelling husband and a mother to two very active boys. I am a Holistic Health Coach who is passionate about helping others to make healthy and sustainable choices that will benefit their mind, body and the planet. I love food and the social events that surround it, and nothing makes me happier than sharing delicious, nutritious, home cooked plant-based food together with friends and family. I care deeply about the impact I have on this earth, and I want my footprint to be light but my impact heavy.

My story here is based on the following intersectional dimensions of diversity: Beliefs and practices (food preferences)

Here is my story of bias and discrimination...

As a child, I had cereal without milk, bread without butter, and during school lunchtime, was the only child without a carton of milk. I didn't like eggs and was picky about the meat I ate. By the time I reached my mid-30s, I was exhausted. I was experiencing endless bouts of tonsillitis - and all the antibiotics to go with them - hives, fatigue, inflammation and a general lack of energy. After reading stacks of books and numerous blogs about the impact of nutrition, I decided to embark on an elimination diet. After just 14 days, I was sold. I felt like a different person! Boundless energy, brighter eyes, smoother skin, and no inflammation were just a few of the benefits I was experiencing after just two weeks. Apart from my regret at not making the switch to a plant-based diet earlier, I haven't once looked back....and I haven't suffered a bout of tonsillitis since. Despite feeling so much better and knowing that I am doing the right thing for my body and the environment, I have often felt like the 'odd one out' or the 'difficult one' because of my food choices, particularly in social settings.

On one occasion, at a restaurant, I was presented with a dessert with the words "I'm afraid yours doesn't look as good as everyone else's". On another occasion, writing ahead to a restaurant, I was assured that the chef would create something to cater for my plant-based requirements as they had no plant-based options on the menu. On arrival, I was shown the menu and told all the ingredients that could be removed from a dish to make it plant-based but not what they could add in. It was a plate of rather plain vegetables.

At another time, when out for a meal, everyone else had a choice of set menus to choose from ahead of the event. I was told my food choices would be catered for, so I wasn't presented with a choice. I was presented with dish after dish, or should I say, side dish after side dish. I left hungry, disappointed and the joke of the table. At a catered buffet lunch for a meeting about sustainability, I was delighted to see the trays of food labelled "vegan" and shocked when I looked to the other end of the table to see the trays labelled "normal".

Here is how you can be an active ally to someone like me…

I believe that there are many preconceived ideas about vegans when there are actually so many reasons for choosing a plant-based meal. As an ally, make an effort to understand people's food preferences. On both sides, we need to be able to have open, non-judgmental discussions while respecting each other's food choices and the culture, tradition and deeply personal reasons that drive them. We need to be mindful of the terminology 'them' and 'us' that creates a divide. There is always some middle ground and that's what needs to be identified.

As an ally, ask for more sustainable food options on menus in office canteens. In doing so, the workplace can be inclusive to not only vegan/plant-based employees but also the growing number of flexitarian employees who want to eat more sustainably. Making all plant-based options visible, putting them side by side with the animal-based ones, rather than in the "box of shame" can help with being inclusive to employees' food choices. At workplace events, you can be an ally by checking people's dietary preferences and ensuring that caterers and restaurants are well-placed to cater inclusively for the range of people's food choices while ensuring that the food people are getting will be substantial and delicious, and avoid them being the "joke at the table".

5

AUTHENTIC CONVERSATIONS

"Authenticity is simply telling the truth to yourself and others."

MAYA ANGELOU, *American memoirist, popular poet, and civil rights activist*

To be better active allies and achieve inclusive workspaces, we desperately need to be able to have authentic conversations. I recently pointed out a colleague's bias using empathetic questioning and was told "Please end this now." No apology. No self-reflection. No desire to do better. No desire to engage. Sadly, when it comes to addressing biases in workplaces, the lack of willingness to engage in authentic conversations is widespread. Why is that and how do we ensure that we don't end up in a situation, as I did, where the other person simply does not want to engage? What was missing in that recent interaction of mine?

Psychological safety.

Psychological safety is crucial to ensuring that we are able to engage in honest and open conversations about all things DEI. Professor Amy Edmondson, from Harvard Business School, who coined the term, defined it as "a belief that one will not be punished or humiliated for speaking up with ideas, questions, concerns or mistakes, and that the team is safe for interpersonal risk-taking."[65]

At first, being an active ally can feel like we are walking on eggshells.

I have lost count of the number of times I have had White male leaders share that they are scared - scared of saying and doing the wrong thing. Even when they are well-intentioned, they seem to be at the receiving end of harsh criticism and even accused of being non-inclusive. I see fear in their eyes. The problem with this fear is that they stop trying and we end up alienating the very people who we need to step up and be active allies. For us to nurture inclusive workplaces, we need everybody to be an active ally. For everybody to be able to be an active ally, we need psychologically safe workplaces. In such an environment, we may sometimes get it right and have positive allyship experiences, where our behaviours have a positive impact in creating a safe environment for others who may have felt unsafe. At other times, we may fumble and find ourselves in negative allyship experiences, where we may have made mistakes that we need to learn from. This is natural. We need to get uncomfortable first - and go through a period of flux - before we reach a new equilibrium. Remember the pendulum? It will likely swing wildly from one side to another until we reach a state of equilibrium - a new equilibrium. Persevere through this difficult phase, I promise it gets better.

Being an active ally can seem daunting at first, but much like any other learned behaviour, it gets easier as we engage more. In the allyship comfort zone, we have more positive allyship experiences where we are able to behave more consistently and frequently in ways that nurture inclusive workplaces. In this zone, our fear and hesitation reduce significantly, we feel psychologically safe to engage in authentic conversations, and our confidence and comfort with being an active ally increases. Active allyship becomes who we are.

To support each other to reach the *allyship comfort zone* will require a psychologically safe environment in our workplaces. An inclusive organisation is one where everyone is encouraged to address biases and all individuals feel safe to engage in authentic conversations to discover their own biases. In such an environment, both those who are the target of the bias, as well as those committing the bias, are not fearful to have these conversations. For this to happen, there must first be a deep understanding that everyone is biased, and that the journey towards inclusion is one we are all on together. Empathetic engagement and authentic conversations are very useful tools to avoid pointing fingers to avoid the blame game.

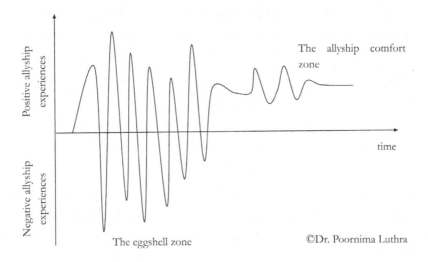

Getting to the allyship comfort zone

In an inclusive culture with psychological safety, biases are openly addressed and minimised through authentic conversations. In such a culture, employees feel that they are able to 'bring their whole self to work', a term that was made popular by Mike Robbins in his 2018 book titled *Bring Your Whole Self to Work: How Vulnerability Unlocks Creativ-*

ity, Connection, and Performance. The idea behind this concept is that each of us has a diverse set of personality traits, backgrounds, skills and circumstances. When we are able to be ourselves in our work environments and not have to leave anything behind, we can give of ourselves fully to the organisations we work for. The challenge? According to a 2020 YouGov study in England, almost one in five workers – about 6.5 million people – feel they cannot be their whole self at work, with people of colour reporting this most frequently.[66]

So how do we nurture inclusive workplace environments? How do we strive for an environment where everyone feels psychologically safe to engage in honest and open conversations to reduce the presence and impact of biases so that we can all bring our whole diverse selves to work?

First, we need to stop avoiding difficult conversations, uncomfortable as they can be. Without open, honest conversations, we will never be able to push the pendulum further and faster towards inclusive workplaces for all. Yes, it may be uncomfortable the first few times we engage in conversations about biases or privilege, but we need to push ourselves and those around us to have those conversations. A key barrier to having these authentic conversations - other than the lack of psychological safety - is the lack of know-how when it comes to the language and vocabulary we can and should use when engaging in dialogues about sensitive issues. However, we need to stop being fearful to talk about difficult bias-related issues simply because we do not have the language framework to do so. Ideally, we should have a deep curiosity to seek out the right vocabulary and develop a deeper understanding on the issues at play. At the same time, there may be times when we may use the wrong language or engage in termite biases ourselves. In psychologically safe environments, mistakes are not punished but seen as an opportunity for growth. In such environments, everyone is willing to engage in constructive dialogues and conversations with the aim of nurturing inclusive workplaces.

When engaging in authentic conversations, there is a real danger of gaslighting someone's experiences of biases. The term gaslighting comes from the title of the 1944 film *Gaslight*, in which a husband uses psychological manipulation to convince his wife that she is mentally unwell so he can steal from her. The term gained widespread awareness in the mid-2010s and is defined by the Merriam-Webster dictionary as "to psychologically manipulate (a person) usually over an extended period of time so that the victim questions the validity of their own thoughts, perception of reality, or memories and experiences confusion, loss of confidence and self-esteem, and doubts concerning their own emotional or mental stability."[67]

Within a workplace context, gaslighting occurs when a colleague or manager manipulates a person to the point that they begin to question their own sanity, memory, or perceptions. The gaslighter can do this by denying past events, downplaying the person's emotions, or retelling events so that the person takes the blame and not them. According to Vicki Salemi, a career expert and coach for Monster.com: "Gaslighting at work is when a person - typically a colleague or manager - invalidates what you know to be true, forcing you to question the facts and, ultimately, yourself and your ability to do your job. In other words, they're twisting (either accidentally or intentionally) information, words and behaviour to make you feel confused, trivialize feelings and block you from success."[68]

According to Dr. Robin Stern's 2007 book *The Gaslight Effect*, there are three distinct stages of gaslighting, though not all gaslighting dynamics will involve all three.[69]

- *Disbelief.* Someone displays gaslighting behaviour. It seems unusual, but you brush it off as a one-time thing.
  A colleague took credit for your idea. When confronted, they deny that such a thing ever happened.
- *Defence.* After a few more instances of gaslighting, you start to defend yourself.
  The person goes to your supervisor with complaints about you harassing them over 'stealing' their ideas.
- *Depression.* Eventually, you accept their version of reality to avoid conflict and do whatever you can to earn their approval. But this denial of reality drains your energy, disconnecting you from yourself and leaving you feeling low and hopeless.
  You start to wonder if it was your idea in the first place or perhaps you were remembering incorrectly.

To foster psychological safety, being aware of gaslighting is key. So what can we do as active allies to ensure that we are not gaslighting someone's experience so that we can engage in authentic conversations? Avoid saying or doing the following:

- Denying a colleague's recollection of events.
  "That's not what happened, you must be mistaken."
- Dismissing and belittling a colleague's experience.
  "It is not a big deal. You are being overly sensitive and crazy."
- Casting doubts over a colleague's feelings, behaviour and state of mind.
  "Are you sure about this? You seem to be overthinking this." or *"X is mistaken about what happened."*
- Openly shaming a colleague in meetings or in front of clients.

- Retelling events or twisting facts to shift the blame to a colleague.
- Insisting that you are right and refusing to consider a colleague's facts or perspective.
- Insisting that your colleague said or did things that they didn't do.
  What about psychological safety amongst teams? At the team level,

Amy Edmondson defines psychological safety as "a shared belief held by members of a team that the team is safe for interpersonal risk taking."[70] Here are some ways in which teams can engage in authentic conversations in an environment of psychological safety:

- *Prioritise* engaging in honest and open conversations about DEI. Establish a shared understanding as a team that it is important to be able to openly discuss challenges being faced with inclusion and the need for greater diversity, bias or privilege and equity.
- *Focus* on learning and having a growth mindset as a team. Repeatedly reiterate that everyone is biased to reassure team members. Emphasise that everyone is there to learn to become more inclusive. Communicate that team settings are a great platform to work on reducing our biases and to become aware of the biases we didn't know we even had, our unconscious biases.
- *Establish* team norms on addressing biases. Have an action or a phrase that everyone uses when a bias is noticed by any team member. For example, it could be raising a yellow card placed on the table or having a code phrase like "oops". Also have a phrase that team members can use when their bias is pointed out like "good catch".
- *Engage* in continuous bias awareness interventions. These could take the form of workshops or training sessions, keep-

ing in mind that a one-off bias awareness training session will not be effective in nurturing inclusive workplaces. Addressing biases through workshops/training sessions need to be seen as part of an ongoing program of nurturing inclusive workplaces. Remind each other that it has taken decades for us to layer on biases, and that it will take time to peel them off. In between training sessions, teams can read an article on biases once a week or month and devote the first few minutes to hear reflections from a few team members to keep honest introspection going.

- *Set* aside time to have honest and open conversations.

  When a concern or bias is raised, resist the temptation to get back to "work-related" tasks instead. Consciously engage in authentic conversations about what happened, being careful not to dismiss or get defensive. When team members become defensive or dismissive, direct them back to focus on being more inclusive. Also, ensure that the person raising the concern does not get interrupted while sharing their concern.

Authentic conversations means:
- Understanding the role of psychological safety in being able to have honest and open conversations.
- Understanding that to get to the allyship comfort zone takes time and effort.
- Having an understanding of the issues at hand and the needed vocabulary to engage in difficult conversations.
- Understanding what gaslighting is and avoiding gaslighting at all costs.
- Establishing a team charter to foster psychological safety.

Reflecting on gaslighting

Gaslighting is an uncomfortable term. For some, it may also be a relatively new term. So spend some time reflecting on your own experiences with gaslighting, whether you feel you were on the receiving end of manipulation, or the gaslighter. This is a personal reflection. You don't need to share this with anyone but be honest with yourself.

- ☐ *Have you ever been gaslit?*
- ☐ *Have you ever been the one gaslighting a colleague?*

If you need help to determine if the answer to either of those questions is true, take a look at the list below.

- ☐ Has your recollection of events been denied, or have you denied a colleague's recollection of events?
  Reflect: Has this been said to you, or have you said this to someone else - *"That's not what happened, you must be mistaken."*
- ☐ Have your experiences been dismissed or belittled, or have you dismissed or belittled a colleague's experience?
  Reflect: Has this been said to you, or have you said this to someone else - *"It's not a big deal. You are being overly sensitive and crazy."*
- ☐ Have you had doubts cast about your feelings, behaviour and state of mind, or have you cast doubts over a colleague's feelings, behaviour and state of mind?

Reflect: Has this been said to you, or have you said this to someone else - *"Are you sure about this, you seem to be overthinking this?"* or *"You must be mistaken about what happened."*

☐ Have you been openly shamed in meetings or in front of clients, or have you openly shamed a colleague in meetings or in front of clients?

☐ Have you had events or facts retold or twisted to shift blame to you, or have you retold events or twisted facts to shift the blame to a colleague?

☐ Have your facts or perspectives been refused to be acknowledged, or have you insisted that you are right and refused to consider a colleague's facts or perspective?

☐ Have you been accused of saying or doing things you didn't do, or have you insisted that your colleague said or did things that they didn't do?

Establishing your DEI team charter

Authentic conversations require psychological safety between team members. With your team or with colleagues that you work frequently with, establish a team charter for what psychological safety will look like so that you can engage in honest and open conversations about all things DEI, including bias and privilege. Use the guide below to help you.

Step 1: Articulate, as a team, why engaging in honest and open conversations about DEI is a priority for your team. Ensure that there is shared understanding and buy-in from team members.

Step 2: Reiterate that everyone has biases, and that learning and a growth mindset are at the heart of difficult conversations.

Step 3: Establish a set of team norms for when biases are noticed.

Step 4: Create a calendar of team activities that increase awareness about bias and empower team members to address bias at the individual, team and organisational levels. These can coincide with other company-wide events and can be done collaboratively with the team's HR business partner.

Step 5: Agree on allocating adequate time periodically to address any DEI concerns from team members. Be specific and intentional about when these sessions will be held, and what the purpose of these sessions will be.

Saroni Roy (She/Her)

I am a multi-hyphenate, Indian-origin Australian actor based in Sydney. I am the co-chair of Equity Diversity at Media, Entertainment & Arts Alliance (MEAA), keynote speaker, creative consultant, PR & media professional, and social entrepreneur. I champion Diversity, Equity & Inclusion and am also the first Indian-origin Australian woman to be elected as Federal Councillor of the National Performers Committee - MEAA.

Born in Jamshedpur, India, I moved to Mumbai for my University Degree and worked in Mumbai for over a decade as a journalist. Hailing from a Bengali-Brahmin family of artists and singers, performing and visual arts has always been a way of life for me. I got my training in Indian semi-classical singing and in several dance forms namely Kathak, Bharatnatyam, Odissi and Flamenco from the age of three.

In 2014, I moved to Sydney, the land of the Gadigal people of the Eora Nation and have since lived in Wangal land. I am a cancer-survivor, facing multiple invisible disabilities like endometriosis, femoral tumour, essential thrombocythemia, which puts me at risk of leukaemia and bone marrow cancer, chronic excruciating pain in my left leg for the past 7 years which only recently was diagnosed as being caused due to degeneration in spine. These have had an impact on my fertility and mental health. I'm a Body-Activist, changing the narrow ideals of beauty, destigmatizing and democratising mental health, creating more access to visible/invisible disability, shattering the glass ceiling in several ways. In 2020, I christened my diversity, sustainability & social justice initiatives as Saroni Roy Foundation (SRf) and SRf Creatists, perpetuating socio-economic and environmental well-being, creating a more peaceful and inclusive 'one world' to live and love.

My story here is based on the following intersectional dimensions of diversity: Gender - Disabilities - Physical appearances - Educational background - Experiences and skills - Personality - Race, ethnicity and culture - Beliefs and practices - Marital and parenthood choices - Socio-economic background

Here is my story of bias and discrimination...

From a very young age, I was told by my mum to take care of my brother who is 6 years older than me. I was expected to be more understanding, be more mature, be more responsible, and be motherly. I feel I somehow never got to be a child. I never thought about myself or my needs. The women in my life - my grandmum and all the women in my family - would constantly feed my mother with these ideas and notions.

I grew up to be a "goody-two-shoes" teenager - an ideal daughter, always composed, graceful, mature, quiet, shy, introverted and great at academics, the arts, cooking, household chores, 'puja paat' (religious practices). I felt and behaved much older than my age. I could never do anything wrong or immoral as per the Indian society's rules and norms. I was always told to be "lady-like" and not laugh out loud, not show too much teeth, speak softly, not have a boyfriend, etc. Once I reached puberty, I was not allowed to wear western outfits anymore, basically preparing to be the ideal Indian daughter-in-law. And suddenly, I was told that I look older than my age. When I was in high school, everyone at public gatherings would be discussing that I look like a 25-year-old woman! I was bullied and teased, called names by everyone including doctors, as being fat or overweight. I was even called an "elephant". I was not fat or overweight as per my height at that age. I was taller than most of my classmates. I simply didn't fit into their mould of a petite Bengali girl. I only became overweight after cancer - thyroidectomy, when I lost my thyroid gland. That is when weight & energy level management and maintaining hormonal balance became challenging.

When I moved to Mumbai after high school for university, I lived all by myself in a huge cosmopolitan city. I faced constant bullying from my roommates and hostel mates and was mocked for my clothes, my naivety, my accent, my voice, my body, everything I was. I was from a small town like Jamshedpur. I wore mostly salwar kameez (Indian traditional clothes), didn't know how to wear makeup, or style my hair, I was a village girl to them. I have a deep voice, so I was told I try to attract men by sounding sensuous and sexual. I have a British accent to English, so I was told I'm trying to attract men by putting on an accent. I had a curvy, toned body, and got a lot of attention from men and a lot of times women as well, so I was told I'm constantly trying to attract men with my voluptuous body, and the sexual assaults I faced were due to my body language and my voluptuous body.

In 2013, I was diagnosed with cancer. Yes, it was a big shock, a jolt, but also the biggest turning point in my life! After an invasive surgery, and facing death, I realised that I never lived for myself, never prioritised myself. I was burnt out from conforming to society. I needed to focus on building my relationship with myself. So in 2014, I took a leap of faith and moved to Australia with two suitcases, no job and just enough money to survive a month. In spite of my stupendous educational credentials, I still didn't get a job in Sydney because of a lack of local experience. After applying for over 900 jobs, I took up whatever job I got as a customer service, market researcher.

After a year of shared accommodation, I finally moved into an individual apartment! Along with my job, I started teaching in leading language schools in Sydney. Unfortunately, due to the excruciating pain in my left leg, I was bedridden and had to quit teaching. While bingeing on Netflix, I enrolled in acting classes. It was then that I was able to meet magnificent artists, create timeless works of art, push boundaries, explore new territories, physically and intellectually. It's the one profession which uses each bit of my talent, good and bad genes, optimally and constructively, to portray a character created by someone else, set in another world! I had to completely accept, embrace and cherish everything I am, because the camera captures everything, exactly the way you are right now. It's meditative, and healing. These experiences have motivated me to work to reshape the fashion industry with my body-positivity campaign.

Here is how you can be an active ally to someone like me...

As an ally, create space for vulnerable conversations. For a long time, I didn't open up or talk about my history of cancer or what I went through. The first time I talked about it was my Ms. India Australia beauty pageant speech. Only when I started to share my vulnerabilities and my journey did I actually start to heal. Having an understanding and being able to have deeper conversations about mental health, disabilities that are visible or invisible, wellness and healing mechanisms is crucial.

Also, be sensitive to what I have been through. A lot of people say: "Oh but your cancer was in 2013, so now you're all good right?" Cancer is not a fever, cough or flu that just goes. The pain of healing physically and emotionally from thyroidectomy and thyroid cancer is real. It's not just taking a pill for the rest of your life. It's the invisible disabilities, the underlying health conditions that you go through for the rest of your life. Endometriosis, essential thrombocythemia, femoral tumour, degeneration in my spine. All of this has had an impact on my fertility, a challenging obstetric journey. Imagine how this impacts my mental health? How can you support and provide access to a colleague or team member who's going through these invisible disabilities? That's your EQ or emotional intelligence.

Don't just dismiss me assuming that I can't perform a task because of my invisible disabilities. Don't say "She's always playing a victim" or "If you can't perform this task, someone else will do it! Please take care Saroni, I wish you good health and a speedy recovery!" That is not being inclusive! You just fired me because of my invisible disabilities, and I can't take any action against you because there's no law to protect me and support me with my conditions. When I get into a train, there are seats allocated for persons with disabilities. When I take that seat, everyone looks at me like I am this young and able-bodied person wondering why I would need to sit in a crowded train. Just because my disability and pain are not visible and I'm not in a wheelchair or walking with a stick, don't assume that I don't need a seat.

Instead, find out what I need. At a recent event that I was speaking at, I spoke to the organisers of the conference beforehand to inform them that due to my invisible disabilities, I wanted a chair and a mobile microphone so that I can sit for some time and continue my talk. They very generously called and had a detailed discussion with me about the stage layout, my special access requirements and provided all the support and access that I needed. That is allyship in action.

Sumit Agarwal (He/Him)

I'm not supposed to be alive today.

I was born with Cerebral Palsy and couldn't move 70% of my body. For those who are not aware, cerebral palsy is a condition that leads to impairment of muscular coordination usually marked by development damage to the brain before or at birth. If that sounds too technical, basically I can't use my body or brain. Or at least like most people can.

This led to 4 surgeries, each one more difficult than the last. As someone who grew up isolated, I fell in love with human beings. I have been privileged to forge relationships through my experiences with people from organisations like The United Nations, TiE, Della Leaders Club. I have shared my journey with publications like Forbes, Fortune India, Telegraph, with the hope of creating a world where diversity becomes a norm. I believe in this: Disability ≠ useless.

My story here is based on the following intersectional dimensions of diversity: Disabilities - Neurodiversity

Here is my story of bias and discrimination...

When I completed the 4 surgeries, I was suddenly given a shot at a new life. That is when I realised that I was very different from my peers. I looked different, talked differently, and walked differently because of my condition. Anyone who saw me treated me like I was an invalid person, as if I was broken and needed to be fixed. Every time my parents took me out in my stroller, people assumed I couldn't understand them or hear them - so they spoke to me in slow, baby-talk tones. When medical science couldn't cure my cerebral palsy, I was subjected to humiliation through religious healings offered in temples. It wasn't anyone's fault. They were desperate for a cure and willing to try anything.

When I was about to finally start school, my mother, who was once a successful lawyer, quit her job and single-handedly decided to brave everything coming her way to ensure that my schooling and post-schooling education was in institutions for "normal" children. She endured a lot of objection and backlash from these institutions and people around her. They made suggestions multiple times to place me in a special institution and "be done with it". People saw my education as a bad investment.

But it is my mother's extraordinary grit and resolve that endowed me with all the help required to fortify me emotionally and instil in me the confidence that would enable me to make a difference in the world. When it was time to start my career, my able-bodied peers started collecting cheques, signing bonuses and kicking off their careers. I could not land a job even with a 9.05 cumulative GPA in my MBA & postgraduate program in management (PGPM). After getting rejected from six interviews, not because of my performance, but because of my physical attributes, I began to wonder why should I plead for jobs when I could give others one. To hell with the world - if they don't give me a job, I'll just figure something out on my own.

I took a leap of faith and I decided to start my own PR firm.

It made sense. PR is all about human relationships - and how you leverage them to get what you want. It came to me naturally. During my childhood, I spent months in the hospital with death looming over my head every time I entered the operating room. At these difficult times, I found comfort in the hospital staff and other patients around me and their company. With limited social interactions, I had to work hard to become "normal". Through observation, I understood why people do what they do, what matters to them when they're inches away from death, and why, in the end, we're all just striving to achieve our own individual definitions of "normal". I realized what we are all really looking for is to create an impact. So, I created PR Signal to understand and build relationships that last a lifetime.

Along the way, I've realized that I was never broken or needed fixing, whatever my physical abilities are, my mental abilities were always on par with my peers, I was never in need of anyone's pity or sympathy. It has always been about acceptance and inclusion. I am disabled and that's not a bad thing. I found acceptance through my parents, irrespective of being subjected to the judgment and discrimination from friends and family. Each time I'd enter the operating room, the doctor would tell my mother I might not make it. Each and every single time, my mother would stay up many nights, crying desperate tears with no support in sight. That's why this isn't just about me.

This is for brave parents like mine, with children like me. Through my story, my company, the success we've had, I want to reach them. Reach them, show them, tell them, and promise them that it's possible. That disability is just a perception, that people tend to have their own preconceived notions about my condition.

I have been repeatedly told I should spend my energy on trying to walk or try sporting activities that can benefit my movements, but am I defined only by my ability to move? Can I not have my own aspirations to fulfil? Does that make me lazy and incompetent? Rather than labelling me with your preconceived notion let me choose my own labels. If I have never been ashamed of my disability, you certainly don't need to be.

You don't have to give up hope, people like us can strive to be better than we're supposedly destined to be. If I reach even one, and my story helps them to hold on to hope, to fight, to find freedom through their vulnerability, to not give up on their child, son, or daughter, I'd know my time here was worth it. My journey here......was worth it.

Here is how you can be an active ally to someone like me...
Don't just check boxes, create value.
Don't just hire, give people a place to belong.
Don't just have targets, create culture.

Don't just hire disabled and/or neurodivergent employees with the primary goal of improving diversity, this sets all parties up for disappointment. Without the adequate foundation, diversity goals will stay just that, goals. To make goals a sustainable reality, the foundation of safety, inclusivity, and accessibility must first be built. Focus on the fact that disabled and neurodivergent employees, when valued and supported, strengthen the culture, creativity, and bottom line.

6
VULNERABLE INTERACTIONS

*"Vulnerability is the birthplace of
innovation, creativity and change."*

BRENÉ BROWN, *American research professor,
lecturer, author, and podcast host*

The very mention of the word vulnerability can make some of us feel uncomfortable. Some would argue that vulnerability is a weakness and has no place in our workplaces and organisations. I beg to differ. Vulnerability is one of our greatest strengths when being an active ally. In her book, *Daring Greatly*, Brené Brown defines the term as "uncertainty, risk, and emotional exposure". She goes on to say, "But vulnerability is not weakness; it's our most accurate measure of courage."[71]

Vulnerability is the discomfort we feel when we step out of our comfort zone. When we are forced to do things differently from the way we have always done them, when we challenge the cookie cutter, or engage in difficult, uncomfortable conversations to support those who are very different from us, that is vulnerability. Vulnerability is about building trust and connection with others whose diversity thumbprints and life experiences look different from ours. It enables us to advance inclusion by building and nurturing supportive relationships with under-represented, marginalised or discriminated individuals or groups.

Two years ago, I was having dinner with my family when my then 11-year-old son, Rohan, was sharing that a guest speaker from

Google had given a presentation at school that day. Without pausing for a moment, I asked "Was he a dad at school?". As the words rolled off my tongue, I was aware of my bias. The wonderful thing, however, was that my son jumped up, pointing it out to me: "Mom, that was so biased of you…and it was a woman!". The somewhat embarrassing part is that I had a very clear image in my head of what the person from Google talking about data looked like. In my mind, he was an Indian man. I could describe exactly what I imagined him to look like, sound like and could even tell you about his likely life story. There I was, my bias laid out on the dinner table for all to see. Even though I was in a very psychologically safe space with my family, having a bias pointed out to me still made me feel ashamed. After all, this is what I do for a living. While I am happy my son caught the bias in my comment, it was still uncomfortable. I had to accept the vulnerability of admitting the mistake and sit with it. My response to him was: "Good catch sweetheart, good catch". We all have biases, even those of us who engage in this work every day. If only we would give ourselves the permission to be as vulnerable at work as we are at home.

Recently, during a DEI panel discussion, a senior leader of a company shared a biased comment she had made to her entire team. During an end of year online meeting in 2021, she signed off by wishing everyone on the call "Merry Christmas". Her husband, who had been in the other room listening in - the unwanted side effects of working from home perhaps - came over and asked her if the session went well. This senior leader energetically responded by highlighting how thrilled she was to end the year on such a high note. He then asked: "You wished everyone Merry Christmas. Do you think everyone on the call celebrates Christmas?" To the large audience of colleagues gathered at that panel session, she expressed the embarrassment she felt at the idea that she had said something that favoured one group over another. Not only did she have to sit with the discomfort of possibly offending her colleagues, but also the uncomfortable feeling of having her husband point it out to her. Her response? "Aghhh, that was a rookie mistake. Of course not. I should have said 'Happy Holidays!'" In sharing her experience, she emphasised that we all have the opportunity to practise vulnerability and to be open to our biases being pointed out and to learn from those experiences. This leader was not just vulnerable in that moment, but also in exposing herself in sharing the story on the panel.

Stories or personal narratives are powerful. As human beings, it is one way we connect with one another. Stories have always been a part of our existence, from carvings on the walls of caves in the stone age to folklore and mythology through to the real-life stories of people's lives - their struggles and celebrations. Our stories allow us to connect with each other on a much deeper level and they can impact what we say, do and how we think in very profound ways. Stories give us an opportunity to learn from another person's experience and can shape, strengthen or challenge our opinions and values. They are an effective way to enlighten colleagues about diverse perspectives and life experiences. Hearing personal narratives from colleagues, the very people that we interact with daily, can be extremely powerful in shifting mindsets, even in the most resistant of us. Danish author, Isak Dinesen, once said that "to be human is to have a story."

Yet the organisations we work for seem to give weightage to numerical data. Decisions and actions are predominantly based on numbers. Anecdotal, qualitative narratives are often seen as being inaccurate and "weak" sources of data. Stories of bias or discrimination at work are often assumed to be "made-up" or highly subjective, making many of us hesitant to share our stories for fear of those personal stories being dismissed. While storytelling in marketing campaigns has existed for much longer, it is only in recent years that the power of narratives as a tool of persuasion in enabling cultural transformation in organisations has been recognised. We have seen leaders like Sara Blakely, founder of Spanx, use storytelling to explain how she came up with the shape-wear product.[72] Apple's CEO, Tim Cook, told his story of the decision to come out as a gay man, confiding that even though he is a very private person, he recognised that he owes it to others, especially the LGBT youth, to bring his whole person.[73] I have been inspired, like so many other women, by Indra Nooyi's candid sharing about the difficulties of balancing the demands of being the CEO of PepsiCo with being a wife, mother, daughter and daughter-in-law.

So while we may be convinced of the rational reasons for being more inclusive - the business case that includes improved financial perfor-mance, improved innovation, better individual and team performance - our desire to truly be more inclusive happens when we connect with the need for change at a deeper, more emotive level. So share your sto-ries. Share your stories of bias, discrimination; your stories of when you were an active ally; stories of when you wish you had done things dif-ferently. Keep the story true to what happened and share from your heart. Give yourself permission to be vulnerable. Even the most serious and stoic are often moved by narratives shared by their colleagues. Yes, stories are that powerful.

While stories or personal narratives are one way to help us connect with each other, there are other actions we can take to help us address our biases. On this journey as an active ally, here is a challenge we all face: While we are aware of some of our biases, there are many others we are not conscious of. These unconscious biases influence our attitudes, our words and behaviours, but how do we become aware of something we are unaware of? How do we even know we are being biased?

To address this challenge, having a trusted, diverse group of colleagues with whom we are comfortable asking for feedback and being vulnerable with is extremely beneficial. This group of colleagues becomes our compass as we navigate our own biases. I call this group the *bias compass circle* and it is within this group that we can determine if our actions and ways of thinking or communicating are biased. This circle can provide us with constructive and motivational feedback. If we are being non-inclusive, our bias compass circle can help us understand more about a dimension of diversity we may not yet fully comprehend. This bias compass circle provides a safe zone to be vulnerable and help us become more inclusive. At the same time, giving those in your bias compass circle the mandate to give you feedback implies that they will be more observant themselves, and more likely to act as active allies in contexts beyond the circle.

Bias compass circle

A trusted, diverse group of colleagues with whom we are comfortable asking for feedback about our biases.

What about as a team? How can we be more vulnerable when interacting with others, particularly in team settings? How do we get more comfortable with the discomfort? How do we push ourselves out of our comfort zone?

Here are some tips that may help you get more vulnerable:

- Share personal stories or narratives about incidents when you were biased/discriminatory and what you learnt from them. Show reflection and growth.
- Encourage your colleagues to share their experiences of bias/discrimination with others in their team.
- Engage in uncomfortable conversations about bias and discrimination as a team. Talk about the elephant in the room. Sit with the discomfort. Use the tools described in the previous chapter on Empathetic Engagement to help you with this.
- Find your bias compass circle. Identify colleagues who you believe can help you become more aware of your biases, and with whom you can get vulnerable.
- Spend some time reflecting on how you interact with the team members and colleagues that you most frequently work with, how you are perceived by them, and how the way you interact differs from the way they do.
- Do the inclusive thing. When given a choice, do what will add value to the team from embracing diversity. Break away from the cookie cutter. Push the pendulum the other way.

Vulnerable interactions means:
- Understanding that vulnerability is a strength.
- Stepping out of your comfort zone and sitting with the discomfort of that.
- Starting small and being courageous.
- Finding your own ways of showing vulnerability with colleagues.
- Establishing a bias compass circle for yourself.

Being vulnerable through stories

Identify an experience with bias/discrimination that you can share with your team members, close colleagues or a wider audience at an appropriate time. What would you share? To help you with this, here is a list of guiding questions: What happened during this incident when you were biased or when you felt discriminated against? How did you find out that you were biased or discriminated against? What did you do? What was your response? What did you learn from that? What impact did this incident have on you? Make notes below to help you remember what to focus on when you have the opportunity to share this story.

....

....

....

....

....

....

....

....

....

....

....

....

Understand your Cultural Thumbprint™

Your Cultural Thumbprint™ is your individual cultural identity. The elements of the cultural thumbprint are based on the work of Erin Meyer, Geert Hofstede and Edward Hall as well as my own work with thousands of university students and corporate trainees.

It defines who you are across a set of cultural elements. It is a reflection of your life's influences and experiences; and is some combination of the cultural backgrounds of your parents, the national culture you grew up in, the education systems you were educated in, your personality, your religious or spiritual beliefs and values, the cultural background of your partner or spouse, which countries you have lived in, the culture of the companies you have worked for, and so on.

Your cultural thumbprint is complex and absolutely unique to yourself. No one else in your workplace has the same cultural thumbprint because no one else has had the same life influences and experiences. Even within the same family, no two people have exactly the same cultural thumbprint; we all internalise our life experiences differently. Your cultural thumbprint evolves over time as you acquire new experiences. By creating our own cultural thumbprint, the hope is to be able to know your cultural identity better and to also reduce the biases and microaggressions we have towards others - recognising that everyone is indeed culturally unique.

To create your own Cultural Thumbprint™ involves three stages.

Stage 1: Create a cultural thumbprint for yourself

Carefully read the descriptions for each of the elements of the cultural thumbprint. For each of the questions on the template, indicate with a dot where you lie along the continuum. When all nine questions have been answered, join the dots to complete your own unique cultural thumbprint.

When creating your cultural thumbprint, keep the following in mind:

- This cultural thumbprint is for yourself at work. For some dimensions, we may place ourselves differently on the continuum in our personal lives.
- Ask yourself: "What represents me best and most frequently at work"? While we all adapt continuously to situations and the people we work with, we also have a dominant way of behaving. Place yourself on the continuum where you would prefer to act.
- Be honest with yourself. This is an opportunity to reflect upon your own cultural identity without judgement. There are no rights and wrongs here.
- Keep in mind that your cultural thumbprint will change over time based on your work and life experiences. Revisit and redo your cultural thumbprint every 3-5 years.

Elements of the Cultural Thumbprint™

How do I communicate with others? Low context or high context
- In low context communication, communication is simple, precise, and clear. Things are understood at face value and paraphrasing, or clarifications are encouraged.
- In high context communication, communication is subtle, nuanced and often made up of many layers.

What is my attitude to time? Monochronic or polychronic
- In monochronic attitudes to time, scheduling and sequential planning of events and meetings are preferred. Last minute changes to planned actions are not preferred and even frowned upon. Deadlines and milestones are strictly adhered to. Punctuality is valued.
- In polychronic attitudes to time, timelines are more fluid and flexible. Events, deadlines, and milestones are approximate and subject to change.

How do I build trust with others? Assumed or socialised
- In assumed trust building, trust is presumed because of the working relationship between colleagues regardless of hierarchical positions. "I work with you, I trust you."
- In socialised trust building, trust is built over time through frequent and consistent interactions within the workplace environment as well as outside.

How do I manage disagreement? Confrontational or non-confrontational
- When managing disagreement, those that are confrontational are comfortable in engaging in debate and disagreement, and in fact

view the rich exchange as a means of building trust in the relationship. Within this confrontational approach to disagreement, those who are more emotionally expressive tend to use a louder tone, stronger language and even large hand gestures to get their view across to the other party. In contrast, those who are more emotionally inexpressive, may use strong language but in a calmer tone with less hand gestures.

- When managing disagreement, those that are non-confrontational do their best to avoid situations where conflict and disagreement may arise.

How do I provide negative feedback? Direct or indirect

- When providing direct negative feedback, the feedback is communicated upfront and clearly highlighting the areas of improvement needed. The receiver of the feedback walks away having clearly understood what was not done up to expectations.
- When providing indirect negative feedback, the feedback is packaged and hidden in between more positive feedback and requires the receiver of the feedback to unpack the layers and sift through it to get to the negative feedback.

How do I persuade others? Why-first or how-first

- When using the why-first approach to persuading others, the reason and rationale is explained first before presenting the suggestion, recommendation, or plan of action.
- When using the how-first approach to persuading others, the suggestion, recommendation, or plan of action is presented first before the reasons behind it are explained.

How do I lead others? Egalitarian or hierarchical

- In egalitarian leadership, the power distance between a line manager and team member is very low, and communication across the flatter structures can skip hierarchical lines.
- In hierarchical leadership, the power distance between a line manager and team members is very high, and communication needs to follow strict hierarchical lines.

What motivates me? Individual goals or group goals

- Those motivated by individual goals are motivated by personal rewards and benefits, seeking opportunities to fulfil those individual aspirations.
- Those motivated by group goals are motivated by common goals, seeking opportunities to work collectively to achieve community aspirations for the collective good.

How do I make decisions? Consensual or top-down

- In consensual decision making, input from all relevant team members are sought and agreement has to be reached before actions are taken.
- In top-down decision making, leaders or managers take decisions and inform relevant team members of the decision and the next steps of action to be taken. There is little or no input from team members in the decision-making process.

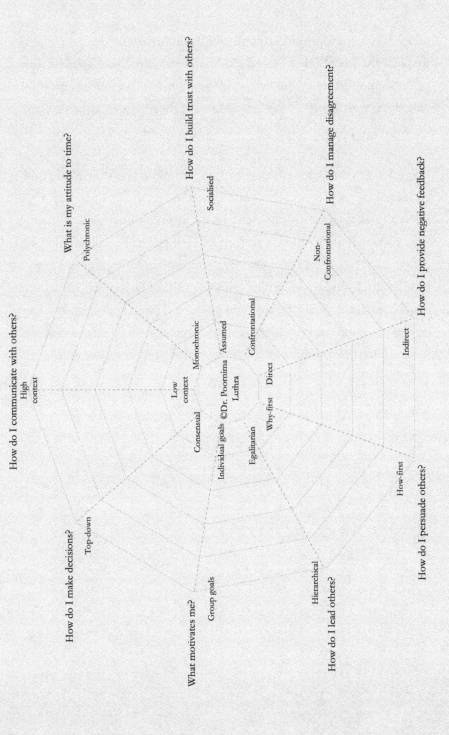

Stage 2: Ask for anonymised cultural thumbprints of you

Request the people that you work closely with to do an anonymised cultural thumbprint of you using the thumbprint on the next page. Provide them with a copy of the explanation of the nine elements. This can be helpful in providing insight into how others view you.

Stage 3: Compare your cultural thumbprint with team members and colleagues

The cultural thumbprint provides an opportunity for teams to create their own individual thumbprint, and then engage in a vulnerable and constructive team session to understand each other's cultural identities. The focus should be on the relative position of yourself with your colleagues, rather than the absolute position. This exercise can be very powerful to unpack the differences and similarities, as well as provide insight into the dynamics within the team and between colleagues.

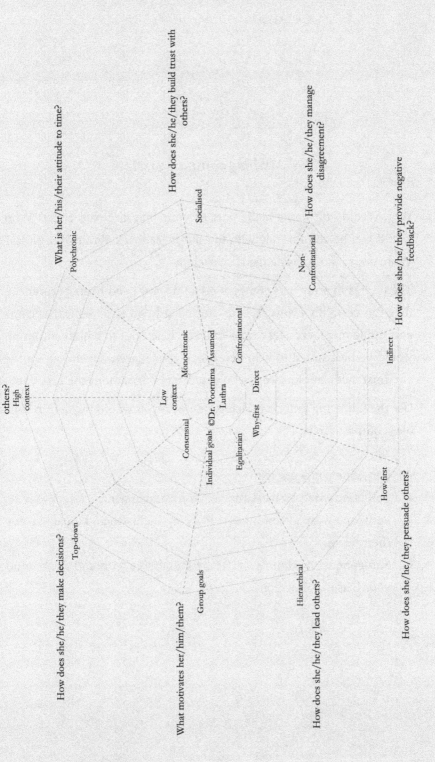

How does she/he/they build trust with others?

How does she/he/they manage disagreement?

How does she/he/they provide negative feedback?

What is her/his/their attitude to time?

How does she/he/they communicate with others?

How does she/he/they persuade others?

How does she/he/they make decisions?

What motivates her/him/them?

How does she/he/they lead others?

Socialised

Non-Confrontational

Polychronic

Confrontational

Monochronic   Assumed

Indirect

High context

Low context

Direct

Individual goals ©Dr. Poornima Luthra

Why-first

Consensual

Egalitarian

How-first

Top-down

Group goals

Hierarchical

My bias compass circle

Who would you invite to be part of your bias compass circle? Who would you be comfortable with to ask for feedback about your biases? Write their names inside the circle below.

The names in your bias compass circle do not need to be permanent, they can certainly evolve. You do not need to go to all your bias compass circle members every time. You can reach out to whom you think would be best suited to help you check your biases, depending on the circumstances, but knowing who you can reach out to is the first step.

Use the following criteria to determine who you would invite into your bias compass circle:

- Someone you work with.
- Someone who you trust and are comfortable with.
- Someone with a keen interest in being inclusive and an active ally themselves.
- Someone with whom you can be vulnerable with and don't mind your biases pointed out.

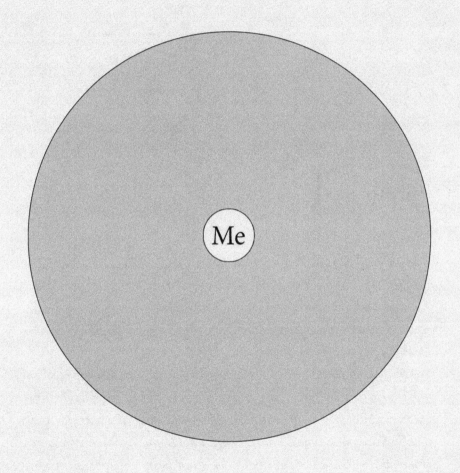

Celia Sandhya Daniels (She/They)

I am an entrepreneur and the Founder and CEO of Rebekon Consulting LLC (c) 2022. I am also a motivational speaker, D&I champion, blogger, composer, musician, photographer, hiker, and filmmaker. I currently reside in southern California with my family. I am an Asian Indian who identifies as gender non-binary, trans fem.

I bring an intersectional blend of ethnicity, creativity, religion, and corporate experience in my "trans-evangelism", as I like to call it. I offer freelance consulting for small to large size companies and volunteers for a few non-profit organisations, churches, institutions, and community resource groups in the United States and India. I am passionate about supporting marginalized communities and individuals by providing them a safe space to address various issues relating to bullying, gender discrimination, medical, behavioral, mental health, and suicidal ideation. I am currently focused on writing policies, educating, and building allies with local communities, businesses, churches, police dept, therapists, doctors, and organisations that fight for civil rights and economic empowerment.

My story here is based on the following intersectional dimensions of diversity: Gender - Sexual orientation - Age - Disabilities - Educational background - Experiences and skills - Neurodiversity - Socio-economic background

Here is my story of bias and discrimination…

My middle name is Sandhya, a Sanskrit name meaning dusk. I have made situations where people have asked if they can call me Sandy because they can't spell or pronounce my name. My response is, "No. That shows that you are not respecting who I am, my ethnicity, my culture, and my value. You're throwing something at me. Who the heck is Sandy? What does Sandy even mean to me?" Those are the kind of conversations we need to bring into the workplace. We should be respecting the person the way they want to be respected.

Growing up as a lonely closeted trans-child in a conservative middle-class Christian home in Southern India, I faced many challenges with mental health, gender dysphoria, and socialising in my family, work, school, and community both in US and India. I also faced significant discrimination after coming out.

Let's start with bathrooms at work. I want to know where I can go to use the bathroom/restroom, somewhere that is safe. Some companies respond with, "I don't know. You can use the women's bathroom if you want because you're dressed like a woman." That is not inclusion, it is tolerance.

Once, when I joined a company, during the onboarding, they were concerned with how to onboard me. This was despite the fact that it was a company with a focus on equality, and pride flags flying all over during the month of June. They didn't have the policies in place to onboard a person after they transitioned from the previous gender. It was not easy for them.

When I'm on a phone call, I have had people on the other side of the call stop me and ask, "Am I talking to Celia?" I reply, "I'm Celia." They then comment, "You sound like a man." To which, I respond, "I'm transgender." I really don't want to keep reminding people that I'm transgender. I want to be able to bring my whole self to work.

Once, at a business networking event, an older man (unknown to me) came up to me with a drink in his hand….

Man: Nice dress.

Me: Thanks (smile)

Man: So… have you done surgery?

Me: No. Not planning to. But why do you ask?

Man: You look like a woman, but you are trans, right? Just curious.

Me: Asking a trans person about their surgery can be very inappropriate.

Man: Look, I don't see anything wrong in asking? I have asked other transgender women.

Me: Well, have you done a vasectomy?

Man: (Serious face) What? Why would you ask such a stupid question?

Me: Just curious. What's wrong in asking? (smile).

Man: (Laughs), hey you got me there…I see your point…that's interesting. (Slowly nods his head).

We ended up chatting about our business and family.

Here is how you can be an active ally to someone like me...

As ALLIES to the Transgender, Gender Diverse, and Intersex (TGI) community, I, Celia Sandhya Daniels, suggest that you need to:

A: Acknowledge your privilege to help our community.

L: Listen to our stories and experiences without assuming.

L: Learn to Unlearn things you may have grown up with.

I: Instigate tough conversations and decisions supporting the TGI Community.

E: Educate yourself and educate others.

S: Support by being involved.

Many trans and gender non-binary individuals don't like to talk about surgery: Not all of them go through medical transition. Bringing up such a conversation can be insensitive and gender dysphoric. It also invalidates them from the cisgender lens. If you want to ask someone about their transition, first listen to them, get to know them, and then bring it up in a polite way. "Hey, I would like to educate myself as an ally. Would you mind if I ask something personal about your transition?"

Don't compare Trans and gender non-binary individuals with cisgender men or women: A woman once told me, that I look like any other Asian cisgender woman, and I shouldn't be worried that I am trans. I said thank you and corrected her politely. Though it seemed like a compliment, it is being dismissive of our existence and putting us into binary boxes.

If you make a mistake, apologize and move on: If you offend a trans or gender non-binary person because you asked a wrong question, just say, "I am sorry, this is a new area for me, and I am learning" and move on. They'll be fine.

Fatima Mohammed (She/Her)

At the request of the contributor, a pseudonym and description (provided by the contributor) have been used.

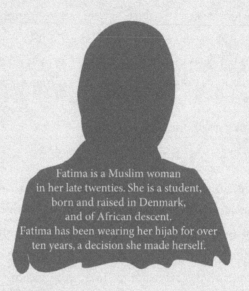

Fatima is a Muslim woman in her late twenties. She is a student, born and raised in Denmark, and of African descent. Fatima has been wearing her hijab for over ten years, a decision she made herself.

I'm a woman born and raised in Copenhagen, Denmark and I identify as an African Muslim. I grew up in Nørrebro, an area where I have always been surrounded by different ethnicities and cultures. I am currently pursuing my Bachelor degree in business administration in Denmark.

My story here is based on the following intersectional dimensions of diversity: Gender - Race, ethnicity and culture - Beliefs and practices (religious beliefs, clothing) - Socio-economic background

Here is my story of bias and discrimination...

Most of the biases I have experienced have been due to my Muslim background as I am a visible Muslim woman who wears hijab. I have experienced that people assume that I am a supporter of ISIS, but also that people tend to stare at me because of my hijab, because I look different from others around me. Living in Nørrebro all of my life means that I feel that I have been very sheltered. I knew that it would be difficult for me to get a job due to my hijab.

However, the first time I experienced outright discrimination at an institutional level was during my studies when I was defending my thesis on diversity and inclusion within the recruitment process. It was obvious from the beginning that the censor and supervisor were very biased, which resulted in my friend and I, who are both people of colour, getting a different grade compared to our third group member who is White. I'm not the type to complain, but this felt very wrong as my friend and I got the same feedback - we were told that we were being too subjective, even though that was in line with our chosen theory.

Here is how you can be an active ally to someone like me...

Learn to listen, ask questions, research, but also do something active and speak up if you see something that isn't right when your friends have experienced bias/discrimination. For example, in my experience above, the White student should have pressured the censor and supervisor to be fair, and should have supported us by speaking up more and helping us through the complaint process against the supervisor and censor. Instead, the student was very hesitant and resistant to get involved to any greater extent. The worst thing you can do is stay quiet. Avoid being a bystander.

Phaedria Marie St. Hilaire (She/Her)

I am Female, Black, Caribbean, Heterosexual, Mother, Married, Wife, Christian (Catholic), Ivy-league Educated, Life Scientist, Pharmaceutical Business Leader, Able-bodied, Tall, Middle-Aged, Introvert and Middle-class.

My story here is based on the following intersectional dimensions of diversity: Gender - Physical appearances - Race, ethnicity and culture

Here is my story of bias and discrimination...

When I studied at a University in the US, in my Chemistry class, the other (White) students assumed that I was only able to attend because I had received a basketball scholarship. Here is the thing - I had been awarded a scholarship on the basis of my academic merit and could not even play basketball. They did not want to partner with me for Chemistry experiments, and quickly selected each other. Then there were three of us left and we formed a motley crew - myself, a young woman of mixed parentage (Japanese and White American) and a White male who was German (had moved to the US to study) and had a deformed left hand. We aced the class and then the others wanted to work with us. Why do we constantly need to prove that we are competent and that we belong?

Fast forward to Denmark and working at a pharmaceutical company as Principal Scientist. One day, while sitting in the break room, a White female colleague enters, goes to the coffee machine and then makes a loud, clearly irritated sound. She then turns to me and tells me in an irritated manner that the coffee machine needed coffee. She had spoken in Danish and at that time my Danish was not that great, so I had had to ask her to repeat what she said in English. When I realised what she wanted, I just told her that she can leave a note on the machine, and I walked out of the room.

Finally, this one happens a lot. When I walk into a meeting with my employees and I am the decision maker, far too often the other persons present in the room initially pose questions to and ask directions from my employees who are White male or female. They just don't expect the decision maker to be someone like me!

Here is how you can be an active ally to someone like me...

Do not be silent; have the courage to speak up and ask questions when bias and injustice is observed. Be curious and express concern; ask me how I am feeling. Seek to understand; ask me if you are unsure. It is okay to ask. I will not be offended if you are genuinely seeking to understand.

7
COURAGEOUS RESPONSIBILITIES

*"When the whole world is silent,
even one voice becomes powerful."*

MALALA YOUSAFZAI, *Pakistani activist for female
education and the 2014 Nobel Peace Prize laureate*

Be that one voice and do the inclusive thing. Active allyship needs you to be courageous and take on responsibilities to challenge the way things have "always been done"; to look beyond the cookie cutter; and to push the pendulum the other way. While it may seem like an insurmountable challenge to change your entire organisation - especially if you work in a large one - start within your own sphere of influence. Everyone has a sphere of influence, whether it is the colleague at the next desk, your office lunch mates, or the team you manage. Start small but start. Don't let the mammoth nature of making our workplaces more inclusive prevent you from making change happen within your sphere of influence.

So how can you challenge the cookie cutter and help the pendulum swing the other way? Through courageous responsibilities.

Start with inclusive communication. The words we use - written or spoken - have an impact on others. Words matter. So take on the responsibility of making conscious efforts to ensure that what you write or say is being inclusive to all. When in doubt, always check in with your bias compass circle. Active allies make conscious efforts to have an inclusive communication style. This includes using audience-centred language

- where active allies analyse their audience to determine the content, language usage, and listener expectations - which demonstrates a deep understanding of DEI and goes a long way in showing not only that they care, but that they are determined to create an inclusive culture.

Inclusive communication begins with day-to-day conversations at lunch, by the coffee machine and during meetings. Here are some ways to be more inclusive in those contexts:

- Avoid using language that is gender-biased. For example, using phrases like "mankind", "man the door", "hey guys", "run like a girl" or "she's got balls", or addressing a female board chair as "chairman".
- Engage in topics of conversation and ask questions that you would with anyone, not just people who identify with certain dimensions of diversity. As a general rule of thumb, avoid asking any questions that you would not feel comfortable being asked yourself. Ask yourself: "Would I be comfortable with this question being asked of me?"
- Avoid conversations that highlight differences. For example: "Why do you wear a hijab/turban?" Quench your deep curiosity through reading credible external sources that will provide you with the answer to such questions. Engage in topics of conversation that do not put the other person in the spotlight by having to justify their life choices, who they are or where they come from.
- When asking a question, let the other person be in control of how they choose to answer. Avoid follow-up questions that question their response. For example, following up the response to the question "Where are you from?" with "Where are you actually from?"
- Beware of termite biases that get embedded in casual comments, humour and compliments like the examples in Chapter 4 on Empathetic Engagement.

- Avoid interrupting others, taking credit for someone else's ideas and resist the temptation to assume others don't understand something requiring you to explain things to them.

- Avoid communicating surprise when someone acts or speaks in a way that you were not expecting them to do so. Instead, when you notice that surprised thought, make a mental note to challenge your own stereotypes and prejudices.

- Be aware of your body language when speaking with others. When engaging with other colleagues by the coffee machine, always have an "opening" in the circle for others to join in. Gesture to others around to join the conversation. At lunch, be mindful of the way you are seated to avoid creating "body walls" (having your back facing an open seat next to you) that prevent others from joining in the conversation.

- Consciously choose to add your pronouns to your name (she/her; he/him; they/them). This could be in your email signature or when signing off with your name at the end of an email or text to a colleague. It could also be when writing your name in presentation slide decks. This helps to make it safe for - and acts as an invitation to - those who wish to make their pronouns known. When communicating to wider audiences whose preferred pronouns are unknown, make an effort to use gender-neutral pronouns - they/them/theirs - to be inclusive.

To help break the bias, here is a list of common phrases that you can easily swap out to be more inclusive. This list is by no means exhaustive. There are of course many others. Keep a look out for them and find inclusive alternatives.

Gender and sexual orientation

Instead of...	→	Try...
Hey guys	→	Hey folks/everyone
Good morning ladies and gentlemen	→	Good morning colleagues/friends/everyone
Woman or man	→	Adult / Person
Mankind	→	Humankind
Business man/ Business woman	→	Business person
Foreman	→	Foreperson
Salesman/ Saleswoman	→	Salesperson
Cameraman/ Camerawoman	→	Camera person
Manned	→	Crewed
Man-made	→	Machine made
Chairman/Policeman/Fireman	→	Chairperson or Chair/Police officer/Firefighter
Manpower	→	People-power/Talent/Employees
2-man job/Middleman	→	Work requiring two people/Middle person
Homosexual/Transexual/Transvestite	→	LGBTQ+/ LBGTQIA+ Transgender people Trans and gender nonbinary folks or folx

Disability & Neurodiversity

Instead of...	→	Try...
Blind recruitment	→	Anonymous recruitment
Mute yourself (when communicating online)	→	Please put your microphone on mute
This is lame/dumb/That is my blind spot/This is our team's handicap	→	This is ridiculous/This is my weakness/This is our team's weakness
Person-first language: emphasises the person, not the individual's disabling or chronic condition	→	Identity-first language: disability is the focus, allowing the individual to own their disability and choose their identity
A person with a (physical) disability /A person with autism		(Physically) Disabled person/ Autistic Person

(It is possible to use both approaches so check in with your bias compass circle or with the person themselves on how they prefer to be identified. Always respect the person's choice.)

Wheelchair-bound person	→	Wheelchair user
Person with blindness/Visually-challenged person/Person who is deaf	→	Blind person/Visually-impaired person/Deaf person

Age

Instead of...	→	Try...
Old-old/elderly/seniors	→	Older employees/Persons 65 and over
Gramps/Grandma, Ok Boomer, Snowflake/ Trophy generation	→	Avoid these completely. Use the person's name and address them respectfully. Avoid making reference to any group through derogatory nicknames.

Race/Ethnicity

Instead of...	→	Try...
I'm a slave to my work.	→	My work seems to have a real hold on me.
These are Chinese whispers/This is all Greek to me/His speech was a double Dutch	→	These are rumours/This is all new to me/I couldn't understand what he was saying
"Borat", "Gora/Gori", "Ching Chong/Chink/Chinky" "Banana/ Coconut/Oreo"	→	Avoid these completely. Use the person's name and address them respectfully. Avoid making reference to any group through derogatory nicknames.

One of the best ways to demonstrate courageous responsibilities is to actively support inclusive initiatives in your workplace. This could involve engaging in conversations on Slack channels/ Yammer or during meetings; or attending events, talks or workshops. Even more effective is helping set up, supporting and participating in Employee Resource Groups (ERGs) for colleagues from under-represented, marginalised and discriminated groups and their allies. Volunteer to be a champion for an ERG. If you are in a position of decision-making power, advocating for adequate financial resources and talent to run the ERGs can be a tangible way of demonstrating this support. Also, make efforts to meet regularly with ERG leads to set collective goals that you and others in decision making roles are held accountable for.

As an active ally, be a role model for others to participate in ERGs. Choose to be part of ERGs that support those who are different from you, those with whom you share few dimensions of diversity. At the ERG events, listen intently and support actively. Don't make it about you; focus on how you can support others. Encourage participation from colleagues, and ensure that the company supports ERGs through adequate funding to carry out their activities and by recognising participation in ERGs in individual's performance conversations.

I am often asked how I feel about ERGs. I wish we didn't need them, but the reality is that we do. The goal may be to have workplaces which are just and bias-free, but we are not there yet. ERGs create safe spaces for colleagues from under-represented, marginalised and discriminated groups to discuss the challenges they face, raise awareness of these challenges to the wider organisation, organise initiatives to reduce the gap in opportunities for growth and development, and collaborate on efforts to address the bias and discrimination they face. However, ERGs are not platforms that "fix the women/LGBTQIA+/disabled groups". They are platforms that empower and educate others with the aim of reducing biases and discrimination. This is equity in action.

To avoid being seen as "exclusive", ERGs - whether they are for women or for members of the LGBTQIA+ community or for the disabled or any other group - should be open to welcoming allies to be a part of the group. We don't want to fight exclusion with exclusion. To move the pendulum further and faster, we need those who are part of dominant groups to step up. ERGs provide a platform for active allies to learn, grow and show support towards those they do not share diversity dimensions with. My hope is that one day we won't need separate programs or special days for certain groups, but unfortunately, we are not quite there yet.

Next, in your own sphere of influence, make efforts to lift others and make space. One of the ways you can do this is to ensure that under-represented, marginalised and discriminated groups are included in decision making processes. To help with this, ask yourself these questions:

"Is everyone who is supposed to be in the room, in the room?"
"Who is missing?"
"Whose perspective, experiences, skills and background are we missing to get a more complete picture and understanding of the issues at hand?"

If you are in a position where you have responsibilities over resources and decisions, being an active ally involves sponsoring colleagues from under-represented, marginalised and discriminated groups. Sponsorship can be understood as a "form of intermediated impression management, where sponsors act as brand managers and publicists for their protégés. This work involves the management of others' views on the sponsored employee. Thus, the relationship at the heart of sponsorship is not between protégés and sponsors, as is often thought, but between sponsors and an audience — the people they mean to sway to the side of their protégés."[74] A sponsor is someone who makes efforts, often behind the scenes, to ensure that high-potential employees from under-represented, marginalised or discriminated groups are given opportunities for career growth and development. Without these sponsors, members of under-represented, marginalised and discriminated groups may never get those opportunities for career advancement.

So, what does sponsorship entail? Rosaling Chow shares the ABCDs of sponsorship:[75]

- *Amplifying:* Sponsors share protégés' accomplishments with others with the intention of creating or increasing an audience's positive impressions of them. A great example is of Sal Khan, the founder of the education site Khan Academy whose site gained immense recognition after Bill Gates - who did not know Sal personally but believed in his product - used an interview to declare that Sal's education site had the potential to change the world.
- *Boosting:* Sponsors boost their protégés by underwriting their reputation and providing a guarantee for the protégé's future success. Boosting can take the form of recommending a protégé for roles and positions in which they would thrive and add value.
- *Connecting:* Sponsors actively facilitate new relationships for protégés, giving them access to people that they wouldn't otherwise be able to be connected with. These connections are seen to be beneficial for the protégé's career growth and individual development. This could take the form of a sponsor inviting a protégé to an exclusive meeting with key decision makers to increase their visibility. For example, when Annie Young-Scrivner, now the CEO

of Godiva, worked at PepsiCo, she benefited from the sponsorship of Indra Nooyi, then CEO, who would invite her to attend meetings in China that proved to be valuable learning and exposure experiences.[76]

- *Defending*: Sponsors challenge the cookie cutter to support those who others may consider a "risky candidate". When a sponsor defends, they address an audience who is sceptical or even dislikes or dismisses the protégé and works to persuade them to change their opinion.

Courageous responsibilities also means mentoring those who are from under-represented, marginalised and discriminated groups (known as mentees) inside or outside your organisation by providing advice, guidance, and support to help them achieve their career aspirations. Mentorship and sponsorship are often confused with each other. Mentorship focuses on "help that a mentor can provide directly, such as guidance, advice, feedback on skills, and coaching, sponsorship entails externally facing support, such as advocacy, visibility, promotion, and connections. Seeing sponsorship as a three-way relationship between sponsors, protégés, and an audience clarifies the difference between it and mentorship."[77]

Indra Nooyi, PepsiCo's former CEO and the first woman of colour and first immigrant to head a Fortune 50 company, writes about the many mentors in her work life in her intimate and powerful memoir, *My Life in Full: Work, Family, and Our Future*. She once famously said, "If I hadn't had mentors, I wouldn't be here today. I am a product of great mentors, great coaching. …Coaches or mentors are very important. They could be anyone - your husband, other family members, or your boss."[78] While Nooyi benefited from these great mentors, she has also been a mentor to many, including customers' children who were planning to study in the US. One of her more well-known mentees, Leena Nair, was appointed the global CEO of French luxury fashion brand Chanel in January 2022 after her 30-year career at Unilever. She is the second Indian-origin woman to take over as a global CEO after Indra Nooyi. In October 2021, when the two women had an interaction to discuss Nooyi's memoir, Nair said, "I'm so proud to call her a mentor and friend...All of you know me as pretty confident. But let me tell you, there have been a couple of times I've asked questions to Indra... 'am I good enough or why me?'. She has given me the proverbial kick in the pants to go and get over myself and get back my confidence and given me the shake-up that all of us need from time to time."[79]

If you find yourself wondering if lifting others and making space for those from under-represented, marginalised and discriminated groups will threaten your own opportunities for career development, remind yourself that DEI is not an *either/or* journey, it is an *and* journey. The benefits of embracing DEI means growth for the organisation, both financially and non-financially, which leads to greater opportunities for all. If, in the very short-term, it seems like those from under-represented, marginalised and discriminated groups are being given opportunities that you are not, remind yourself that this is what equity looks like. These efforts are needed to compensate for centuries of systemic biases that have favoured those with more privilege than others. It can be frustrating. It can make you feel resentful towards those groups. You may feel angry. But remember that the pendulum has to swing the other way before coming to an equilibrium.

Finally, courageous responsibilities means addressing *systemic biases*. We would like to believe that we hire and promote people solely based on hard work and merit, but this is far from what happens in reality.

Systemic biases embedded in workplace structures and processes are a significant barrier to achieving the vision of diverse and inclusive workplaces for all. Unconscious and even conscious biases have affected the way our organisational systems and processes have been set up. Over time, these biases have become systemic in nature. How many times have you heard someone bat away a bias with the excuse "this is the way things have always been done", without genuine critical questioning of the biases that lie beneath? These biases and the consequential inequity - favouring some groups and not others - are especially evident in certain key areas of our workplaces: our hiring and promotion practices; the way we compensate talent and provide benefits; the way talent is managed and led; the opportunities for talent development; and the kind of workplace cultures we have.

Far too often I hear these statements from leaders and HR business partners: "We want to hire diversely, but we don't want to lower the bar" implying that anyone who is different from the cookie cutter is automatically assumed to be lacking in experience and skills, or "We want to be diverse, but we can't find qualified diverse talent" suggesting that there are very limited diverse candidates to be considered for the role. The next time you hear these statements, ask yourself and others these questions: On what basis are we making these statements? What constitutes this "bar" that we are referring to? What are we referring to when we use the word "qualified"? Are we actually referring to the person's experience, skills and educational background or are we using the words "bar" and "qualified" as a synonym for "cookie cutter"? Are we truly casting our net as far and wide as possible to reach out to diverse potential candidates? Have we tried hard enough to recruit talent who do not fit the cookie cutter? Or are these just excuses for continuing to hire and promote talent who fit the cookie cutter?

COURAGEOUS RESPONSIBILITIES

I was struck by the impact of our biases on recruitment processes when a student of mine in Denmark shared an experience of hers. She is a Muslim woman who wears a hijab. She applied for student internship positions - as is common practice in Denmark - in some of the largest Danish companies. She noticed that her peers were getting invitations for interviews, and she was not. Her grades and CV looked very similar to theirs with one difference - her photo (yes, we still have photos on CVs in Denmark) was of her in a hijab. Out of sheer frustration, she took off her hijab, took a new photo, added it to her CV and sent them out. Guess what? Once the hijab was removed, she got multiple calls for interviews. Unfortunately, this is not an isolated incident. Our names, where we live, where we studied, our gender, how we look, our marital and parenthood status amongst others all have a significant influence on whether or not we are given the same opportunities or considerations. Biases exist, and they have an impact on who is hired and who progresses through the corporate hierarchy. Recruiters saw a young woman in a hijab and formed opinions about whether or not she would be the "right" person for the internship - based on nothing more than their biases. Their cookie cutters had no room for hijabs. She was not given the opportunity. This is why it is important to note how biases impact our decision making and therefore lead to inequity in our practices in the workplace.

Beyond the talent management realm, biases have impacted the kinds of products and services organisations offer, the way these products and services are marketed, and who they are marketed to. For most organisations, their products and services are designed for some, but not all; the marketing of these products and services represent some customers, but not all; and this marketing is targeted at some customers, but not all. If we want to be inclusive to diverse customers, this has to change.

So, what is our individual role in making this happen faster?

Here are a few key areas in which systemic biases are embedded where you can challenge the "way things have always been done" or what is considered "normal" or the prototype of the "ideal candidate" who "fits well": talent management, products and services, marketing, communications and customer service. Use the exercise at the end of this chapter 'Challenging systemic bias' to think honestly and critically about where the biases in your team or company lie and make concrete efforts to address them.

Right now, our workplaces are built for some to thrive, but not all. Hopefully one day they will be inclusive to all. Perhaps that day will come sooner if each one of us embraces our courageous responsibilities.

Courageous responsibilities means:
- Being inclusive in your communication.
- Actively supporting Employee Resource Groups (ERGs).
- Lifting and making space for others.
- Being a sponsor and/or mentor for those from under-represented, marginalised and discriminated groups.
- Addressing systemic biases embedded in talent management, in products and services, and in marketing, communications and customer service.

How can I take on courageous responsibilities?

Engage in inclusive communication:

Make a list of words or phrases that you commonly use that have biases embedded within them. Write down what you would replace them with using inclusive words and phrases that you would be comfortable using.

Instead of...	Try...

Participation in Employee Resource Groups (ERGs):

Find out about the existing ERGs in your company. Make a list of ERGs that you would like to be a part of. Are they open to active allies joining? If not, kindly request them to include allies. You may need to reassure them that you come from a place of allyship, wanting to learn, grow and support. Remember to choose to be part of ERGs that support those who are very different from you, those with whom you share few dimensions of diversity. Use ERG events to listen intently and support fervently. Don't get defensive or dismissive. Do not gaslight. Don't make it about yourself; focus on how you can support others. If you are in a decision-making role, reflect on how you can advocate for, champion and be held accountable for the goals of the ERG.

Be a sponsor:

Think about who you would be willing to sponsor - your protégé? Are there members of your team from under-represented, marginalised and discriminated groups who are high-potential talent? How can you provide them opportunities for career advancement? How can you *Amplify-Boost-Connect-Defend*?

....
....
....
....
....
....
....
....
....
....
....
....
....
....
....
....
....
....
....
....
....

Be a mentor:

Think about who you would be willing to mentor. Do you have an internal mentorship program in your organisation that you can be a part of? You can also seek out external organisations that help facilitate pairing you up with a mentee. Your mentee should be someone with whom you do not share many dimensions of diversity with; someone who has very different life experiences from you. What kind of advice, guidance, and support could you give them?

Dismantling the cookie cutter, one crumb at a time

What is your sphere of influence? Who are the groups of people within your organisation you believe you can influence to do things differently?

....

....

....

....

....

....

Think about the aspects of the cookie cutter in your team/organisation that you would like to challenge and reflect on how you may be able to do this. Be specific and as detailed as possible. You may wish to refer back to the exercise 'What does the cookie cutter look like at work?' at the end of Chapter 2 on Honest Introspection.

....

....

....

....

....

....

....

Challenging systemic bias

Here is a checklist of guiding questions for you to ask yourself and your leaders, managers and colleagues to challenge systemic biases, and demonstrate courageous responsibilities. Remember, for the gaps identified, follow up action is needed to be an active ally.

Talent management
Recruitment and selection:

- ☐ Do our job ads have an anti-discrimination statement, showing commitment towards DEI?
- ☐ Is the language we use in job ads gender-, race-, culture-, age -, ability-biased? Have we made efforts to neutralise the language used in our job ads to attract talent from diverse backgrounds to apply?
- ☐ Do our job ads state that having diverse perspectives, experiences, skills and backgrounds is something the company is looking for?
- ☐ Have we advertised for the role as far and wide as possible? Are we going to the same universities and placing the ad on the same job portals? Are we casting the net further and wider; in unusual places/different industries? If not, why?
- ☐ When shortlisting candidates, are we anonymising the CVs and other documents? Are we removing the following identifiers - photo, name, age, gender, address, university name?
- ☐ Is the recruitment and selection panel representative of the diversity we would like to see in the company?

☐ Have all the members of the recruitment and selection panel been through regular bias awareness training?

☐ Are we using structured interview questions for all candidates? Is each interviewer on the panel asking the same question?

☐ Are all candidates having the same recruitment experience? Is there a standard process for all candidates? Are we putting some candidates from under-represented groups through additional rounds of interviews or additional tasks?

☐ Can we do interviews differently from the traditional set-up to be more inclusive to neurodiverse talent? Could we have an activity through which we engage with each candidate in a way that helps remove the stress of eye contact and is more relaxed to enable all candidates to thrive including those who learn and think differently from the cookie cutter way? Are we expecting interviewees to conform to a traditional interview process?

☐ Are we offering accommodations to candidates during the recruitment process and once they are hired?

☐ Do we have a clear criteria-based selection process, one of which is about the diversity of perspectives, experiences, skills and backgrounds that is clearly stated in the job ad? Does the candidate bring something different to the team to add value?

☐ Are we basing our decision on gut feelings that the person will not be a good "fit"? Are we thinking the following: "X seemed too gay". "Y is likely to get pregnant"? Be honest.

☐ Can the recruitment and selection panel justify their choice? Was the person the best qualified candidate who met all the criteria including bringing different perspectives, experiences, skills and backgrounds? How similar is the selected person to others in the team? Does the person fit into the team or organisation's cookie cutter shape? Would the person add real value to the team?

Employee value proposition:

☐ Would a person from an under-represented group want to work here?

☐ Do we conduct exit interviews with people leaving to understand why they chose to leave?

☐ Would someone from Generation Z or Alpha want to work for our company?

☐ If someone from an under-represented group joined, would they feel like they belong? What data do we have from our employee and engagement surveys and inclusion surveys that helped us come to that conclusion?

Talent development:

☐ Are some groups in our company given more career opportunities than others?

☐ Do those from under-represented groups have mentors to guide them?

☐ Are managers or leaders aware of their role as sponsors?

☐ What kind of networking opportunities are there for talent? Would someone from an under-represented group attend them? Do we know why or why not?

☐ Do we have adequate parental leave, grandparent leave, menstrual leave options that are inclusive to all?

☐ Do we offer hybrid, flexible working options? Are managers trained to be supportive of these?

☐ Have we conducted a pay equity exercise to uncover if we have unjustified pay gaps across gender identities, race or ethnic identities, functional groups, etc.?

☐ Have we made efforts to correct pay gaps identified from a pay equity exercise?

Products and services:

☐ Are our products and services catering for a diverse customer base? Is this a conscious choice or not?

☐ How often do we involve diverse customers when collecting feedback on our products and services?

☐ How often do we involve diverse customers when collecting feedback when designing new products and services?

Marketing, communications and customer service:

☐ Would diverse customers see themselves represented in our marketing material?

☐ Are our communications, particularly the language that we use, inclusive to diverse customers?

☐ Are our customer service agents trained in how to engage with diverse customers, or is our customer experience based on a dominant customer segment?

☐ How often do we involve diverse customers when collecting feedback on our marketing campaigns and customer service?

☐ How often do we involve diverse customers when collecting feedback to develop new marketing materials?

Now that you have identified the gaps, what are you going to focus on -
within your sphere of influence - to challenge systemic biases?

....
....
....
....
....
....
....
....
....
....
....
....
....
....
....
....
....
....
....
....
....
....

Hafaz Shah (He/Him)

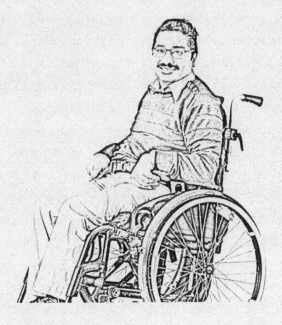

I am a 46-year-old student and am completing my graduate diploma in business administration from Copenhagen Business School. I am ethnically Pakistani and live in Denmark. I have cerebral palsy and therefore can't walk and am in a wheelchair. I am a well-educated, hardworking person.

My story here is based on the following intersectional dimensions of diversity: Disabilities - Educational background - Experiences and skills - Personality - Race, ethnicity and culture

Here is my story of bias and discrimination…

Even though I am highly qualified, I meet a lot of discrimination. I have a bachelor's degree in Data Science from Niels Brock and have had a few short-term jobs at Maersk, IBM and at a job center in Copenhagen. But no one would hire me for a permanent position. For a long time, I applied for Human Resources jobs, without any luck. I finally decided to do a graduate diploma in business administration with a focus on marketing management at Copenhagen Business School (CBS) with the hope of making myself a more attractive applicant for a job.

All people see is my wheelchair. They assume that I can't do the work or need a lot of special equipment or help. On the rare occasion when I get to a job interview, I am often rejected. When I ask what professional abilities I lack, the person on the other end of the phone is silent for a while before replying: "Well we had a lot of talented applicants this round". I have considered not including my disability in my job application, but the problem is that I need to know if I can get into the building in my wheelchair, so it seems impossible to leave it out. The result is that I rarely get called in for job interviews. I also wonder how much of this discrimination is because of my name that reflects my ethnic background. Honestly, I'm afraid that I've wasted the last five years of my self-paid studies at CBS and won't be able to put my skills to good use in a company.

Here is how you can be an active ally to someone like me…

Don't pity me. Hire me because you can see that I'll be an asset to their company. I'm good at recruitment, I can optimise business strategies by reviewing annual reports and finding the gaps and solutions. Also, I'm stable, almost never sick and I have a very positive outlook. Don't assume that I can't do the work. Make an effort to educate yourself about disabilities; ask me directly about what my disability means for my work performance and look at my professional abilities.

Many people are uncomfortable speaking with someone like me, and about disabilities. I think they feel guilty about the biases they have about someone like me. Be an ally - invite me for an interview; talk to me. Don't just see me as someone in a wheelchair. My brain is fully functional. I might spill some coffee on rare occasions if I have a spasm, but that's it. I can be a bit slow at writing on a computer, but I can get a PA to help me with that. I don't use any special equipment and I'm approved for work 24 hours a week. Be an ally by giving me a chance so that I can use my skills and education in a proper way.

Companies and individuals need to walk the talk. All companies talk about social responsibility - now is the time for them to put their money where their mouth is by offering people like me jobs. We need allies who will design workplaces with disabled people, like me, in mind. After all, about 15% of the global population is disabled.

Aram Ostadian–Binai (She/Her)

My name is Aram, CEO and Founder of community and agency The Soulfuls. I am a drop-out electronics engineering student from Danish Technological University (DTU). I have an International Marketing Management degree from Niels Brock, Master of Arts in Media Production from London College of Fashion and Executive Education in Digital and Social Media Strategy from Harvard Business School. After working in the media and creative industries for over 13 years both in Scandinavia and across the UK, USA and Asia, I realised how important it was for my own development to have a strong network of diverse role models.

When I was starting out, I didn't know anyone who could introduce me to someone from the inside. The creative and media industries are arguably predominantly relationship driven. I found that even with the experience of working as a digital editor for a number of publications, the road wasn't straight forward, which is why diverse talent and women often run into closed doors. I am also 36. I am mom to two boys aged 3 and 6. I am a wife. I am an older sister. I am a daughter. I am a refugee.

My story here is based on the following intersectional dimensions of diversity: Gender - Race, ethnicity & culture - Socio-economic background

Here is my story of bias and discrimination...

I was born in Tehran, to parents who raised me to become an independent woman one day. Growing up in a country like Iran, I quickly learnt that becoming an independent woman comes with a price. As I grew older, I realised that my mom had to overcome a lot more challenges than my dad did. While my dad had two shops, I used to hear my mom say to her colleague: "I found the perfect studio. Tried all the tricks, yet they will not accept having my name on the lease. They want a man's name." Being a woman in a country like Iran, by law you are worth only half of a man.

When we moved to Denmark when I was 13 years old, I was told that I had the freedom to be who I wanted to be. Everyone said this. I was told that everything is possible - equal rights for women and men - no matter what your background is.

But my experience was different. I was working hard, studying hard. I was one of the most involved team members and so were many other entry-level colleagues of mine from diverse backgrounds. Yet none of us were making it past the entry level positions. It took me a while to realise that the people deciding what quality looks like, what "normal" looks like... looked nothing like us. We were not White men. This made us unqualified. We didn't know the right things to say, we didn't have the right history or connections with the people in upper management. Worst still - our history got used against us.

10 years ago, I was convinced that only my qualifications, ambitions for my career, as well as my interest in contributing to Danish society, were enough to kick doors open for me. But it quickly dawned on me that bias and lack of representation have formed a narrative - a perception in people - that is harder to overcome than one might think.

In April 2022, I was featured in ELLE Denmark, where the editor's note recollected an episode from many years ago: "For a job interview as a fashion intern at ELLE, she [Aram] was asked if her early marriage was an arranged marriage. Completely irrelevant to the job - in every way - crossed the line, and was judgmental and racist." I did not get the internship then, but today I sit on ELLE Denmark's and Aller Media Denmark's Diversity Board, and ELLE's Editor-in-Chief is among The Soulfuls' mentors. Being a woman, and a woman of colour, is what I call double-trouble. There are at least two glass ceilings to overcome.

Here is how you can be an active ally to someone like me...

If we want to see real change happen, we all need to have and become upstanders. When we are passive and try to "stay out of it", we risk letting bias and discrimination continue to exist. We shouldn't let minorities both deal with discrimination and making change happen, this is a change for all human beings, so we need to come together. We all need to stand up for it because it is not fair and right.

In board meetings or important internal meetings, what I would like to hear allies say: "She is speaking, I would like to hear her out" or "This language can be misunderstood among marginalised groups, can you please rephrase that and be more thoughtful" or "She is bringing a fresh idea to the table, let's give it time/room to explore and circle back with concerns and questions".

Another way to be an ally is to support each other and create networks that voice these challenges in society. As humans, we have always been part of networks. These are usually our close circle. It can be parents who introduce us to their wider network, or teach us about how the world operates at the dinner table, or an uncle or aunt who brings us to galleries or fashion shows, or even in some cases neighbours or classmates we grow up with. Ensure that networks are not an exclusive club. Networks are the most natural thing in the world. And so are women looking after each other. There is an incredible bond between women when women look after each other. Women will be lions for each other! I saw it in Iran. And I see it in The Soulfuls too.

FINAL THOUGHTS

What can I do?

As it turns out, a lot. You can be deeply curious and engage empathetically. You can take part in honest conversations and learn to embrace vulnerability. You can be courageous. You can be authentic. You can become more aware of the biases we all have. You can make a difference. You can be an active ally.

Inclusion needs everyone to step up. Inclusion needs *you* to step up. For far too long, we have been too passive. We have allowed cookie cutters to permeate our workplaces, where they do not belong. Our inaction has helped to keep the pendulum stuck, favouring some but not all. Now is the time for this to change. Cookie cutters don't belong anywhere but the kitchen drawer. The pendulum needs to swing the other way, towards equity. You can make this happen. You can make our workplaces inclusive for all.

In exploring the seven behaviours of active allyship, the topic of *trust* has not yet come up. I find the concept of *trust* truly fascinating. Having lived in parts of the world that view trust very differently - India, Singapore and Denmark - I am acutely aware of how important trust is in relationships at work and in society. Trust can either be built through personal interactions or assumed from the outset of a relationship.

Here's the thing - it is much easier to build or assume trust with people who are more similar to us. This is why we see greater levels of trust in more homogenous societies, and also why it is much harder to build trust with people who are very different from us. My hope and belief is that by being an active ally - by building and nurturing supportive relationships with under-represented, marginalised or discriminated individuals or those with different diversity thumbprints - trust between us will be built across our intersectional identities. When we are an active ally to others, trust is the invisible thread that weaves us together. The resulting tapestry of diversity and inclusion is a beautiful by-product of active allyship.

As I write my final thoughts for this book, the world is in turmoil. The war in Ukraine, an energy crisis, soaring inflation, a looming food crisis, a never-ending pandemic, climate change, widespread inequality, mass shootings and a US Supreme Court ruling overturning Roe v. Wade which protected American women's right to abortion. While this paints a rather bleak picture of the world, it is also a wakeup call. Is this the world we want to hand over to our children and their children? Human history has shown us that in times of crisis, the actions of individuals matter the most. So act we must. Each of us. My hope is that this book has inspired you to act; to be an active ally within your own sphere of influence. We must act to challenge the cookie cutters present in our workplaces, and push the pendulum the other way until it finds its new equilibrium in a world of social justice and equality.

Allyship isn't about perfection, it's about progress. It's about learning and doing better. We may get it right sometimes, but not always. This is new to many of us. We are unlearning our old ways and trying to learn new ways of doing things. We are rewiring our brains from what they have been socially conditioned to think, say and do. As we figure out what works and what doesn't, we need kindness, patience and psychologically safe spaces to be active allies. If we react negatively to people who are genuinely trying, we only foster fear and risk a return to the passive. If we want to engage in active allyship, we need to feel psychologically safe to make mistakes, to learn and keep doing better. We need to allow ourselves to be vulnerable and appreciate that vulnerability in others. If you see a colleague trying to be an active ally, encourage them, cheer them, and help them get better at it. I hope that others do the same for you. Let's focus on celebrating active allyship rather than dismantling the genuine attempts of others. Let's learn together in the spirit of wanting to do better. Being an ally is a lifelong process, after all. This is an art form that you will continuously get better at, now that you have all the tools needed to do your part to nurture inclusive workplaces.

As a final thought, my sincere hope is that one day, my work in the DEI space will become redundant because we would have reached a stage where our organisations are truly diverse and inclusive for all.

Until then, my work continues, and so does yours - do the inclusive thing and engage in *The Art of Active Allyship*.

Poornima

ACKNOWLEDGEMENTS

I am who I am today because of the immense support I have received from many people in my life. I grew up hearing my father saying "expand, expand, expand [your circles of influence]". My father and my mother continue to live these words in their very actions, positively influencing a continuously growing number of people in their lives. I am truly grateful to them for planting this seed of wanting to positively influence others.

Tanuj, my darling partner in life, you have been my rock all these years - thank you for your faith in me. Thank you for so enthusiastically supporting each of my new ideas and projects. For that, and so much more, thank you. To my loves, Rohan and Tejas, thank you for choosing me to be your Mama. Thank you for keeping me on my toes and challenging me to be the best version of myself for you.

To all my fellow DEI practitioners, you inspire me. We all know how tough this work is and how emotionally draining it can be. On those tough days, you are the ones who give me the strength to continue. To all who I have had the pleasure of engaging with over the past few years on this topic, thank you for the deep and powerful conversations. To all the leaders, workshop participants, keynote attendees and students, thank you for engaging honestly and openly with me; for asking the tough questions that challenge me to do better. To all my clients, thank you for your trust in my work and for the many wonderful opportunities to engage with your employees.

Most importantly, a heartfelt thank you to each of you who so courageously shared your authentic and inspiring stories that are featured in this book. You inspire me.

This book would not have been possible without these wonderful, precious, and diverse people in my life. I am grateful.

ABOUT THE AUTHOR

Dr. Poornima Luthra is Associate Professor at the Copenhagen Business School, the author of the book *'Diversifying Diversity: Your guide to being an active ally of inclusion in the workplace'* and the *HBR* article "Do your global teams see DEI as an American issue?". She is also the founder and CEO of TalentED Consultancy and a Tedx speaker. She is an educator at heart, and has spent the last fifteen years teaching university courses in the field of talent management, with a strong focus on Diversity, Equity and Inclusion. Poornima is the recipient of the Professional Women of Colour Denmark 2021 Impact award, and a finalist in the Trailblazer category for Denmark in the 2022 Nordic Blaze Inclusion Awards. Poornima is ethnically Indian, and has lived and worked in Singapore and Denmark.

In 2019, Poornima decided to draw on her years of academic experience to engage more actively in the business world - with leaders and employees - with the vision of making workplaces more inclusive for all. Through keynotes and workshops, Poornima focuses on inspiring inclusive mindsets by expanding the areas of diversity we focus on while empowering individuals to be active allies.

Poornima has worked with a number of international and Danish MNCs and NGOs that include Carlsberg; Carlsberg Foundation; Google; Reckitt; Accenture; KPMG Nordics; Danske Bank; Novo Nordisk; FedEx; Total; Telia; Maersk Tankers; Deloitte; Nothvolt; Ørsted; Medicines sans Frontiers (Doctors without Borders); McCormick APZ; McCormick UK; SimCorp; Visma; IKEA Retail (Ingka Group), Kromann Reumert; and Copenhagen Capacity.

When Poornima isn't engaging in DEI, she relishes spending time with her husband and two boys going for walks and hikes in nature, travelling to explore new countries and cultures, and cooking plant-based meals in the kitchen.

For more information, visit www.talented.dk.

GLOSSARY OF DEI TERMS

Term	Definition
Affinity bias	The presence of affinity bias means that we tend to prefer hiring and promoting people with whom we have a greater similarity of culture and experiences, and with whom we assume we can get along better.
Bias	Inclination or prejudice for or against one person or group, in a way that is considered to be unfair.
Discrimination	Behaviour that treats people unequally because of their group memberships. Discriminatory behaviour, ranging from insults to hate crimes, often begins with negative stereotypes and prejudices.
Diversity	Refers to differences. It is the state of being diverse, and based on the understanding that each person is unique and recognizing that people have differences across a range of human qualities.
Employee Resource Groups (ERGs)	Groups of employees who join together in their workplace based on shared characteristics or life experiences.

Equality	Providing everyone with the same tools, opportunities and support, and does not take into account biases and differences in life experiences.
Equity	Recognising the existence of biases in society and in our workplaces that favour some groups and not others, and makes efforts to compensate for those biases by providing tools, opportunities and support to employees from under-represented, marginalised and discriminated groups.
Homogeneity	The quality of being the same.
Inclusion	A culture in which everyone is respected and appreciated as valuable members, where their voice is heard, and where they feel a sense of belonging.
Intersectionality	The interconnectedness of dimensions of diversity that result in each person's diversity thumbprint and forms the basis of their complex experiences of biases and discrimination. The term was coined by Kimberlé Crenshaw in 1989.
Justice	An environment in which everyone would have fair and equal experiences, and therefore equal access to tools, opportunities and support.

Prejudice	An opinion, prejudgment or attitude about a group or its individual members. A prejudice can be positive, but in our usage refers to a negative attitude. Prejudices are often accompanied by ignorance, fear or hatred. Prejudices are formed by a complex psychological process that begins with attachment to a close circle of acquaintances or an "in-group". Prejudice is often aimed at "out-groups".
Stereotype	An exaggerated belief, image or distorted truth about a person or group. It is a generalisation that allows for little or no individual differences or social variation. Stereotypes are based on images in mass media, or reputations passed on by parents, peers and other members of society. Stereotypes can be positive or negative.

RECOMMENDED SOURCES

Here is a list of my favourite sources on DEI:

Books:
- *Inclusion on Purpose: An Intersectional Approach to Creating a Culture of Belonging at Work* by Ruchika Tulshyan
- *So You Want To Talk About Race* by Ijeoma Oluo
- *Caste* by Isabel Wilkerson
- *It's About Damn Time* by Arlan Hamilton
- *The Allyship Challenge* by Kimberly Harden
- *Biased* by Jennifer Eberhardt
- *Invisible Women* by Exposing Data Bias in a World Designed for Men by Caroline Criado-Perez
- *The First, the Few, the Only: How Women of Color Can Redefine Power in Corporate America* by Deepa Purushothaman
- *Leading Global Diversity, Equity, and Inclusion* by Rohini Anand
- *Diversifying Diversity: Your Guide to Being an Active Ally of Inclusion in the Workplace* by Poornima Luthra

Online resources and podcasts:
- Harvard Business Review, hbr.org
- HBR Women at Work
- HBR IdeaCast
- The Diversity Gap
- Brown Table Talk with Dee C. Marshall and Mita Mallick
- Inclusion Works
- The Will To Change: Uncovering True Stories of Diversity & Inclusion
- The Element of Inclusion
- Code Switch
- Untapped with Tariq Meyers

ENDNOTES

1   Adichie, C. N. (2015). We should all be feminists.

2   https://www.merriam-webster.com/dictionary/ally

3   https://hbr.org/2022/03/do-your-global-teams-see-dei-as-an-amer-
    ican-issue

4   https://www.merriam-webster.com/dictionary/ally

5   https://www.bentley.edu/news/allyship-key-creating-inclu-
    sive-workplaces

6   https://www.bentley.edu/news/allyship-key-creating-inclu-
    sive-workplaces

7   "The Problem with 'Allyship'". National Review. 27 April 2021.; Ow-
    ens, Ernest. "Why I'm Giving Up on "Allies"". Philadelphia Magazine.

8   Schrader, P.G. & Lawless, Kimberly. (2004). The Knowledge, At-
    titudes, & Behaviors Approach How to Evaluate Performance and
    Learning in Complex Environments. Performance Improvement. 43.
    8 - 15.

9   https://www2.deloitte.com/us/en/insights/topics/talent/six-signa-
    ture-traits-of-inclusive-leadership.html

10 https://www.kornferry.com/capabilities/leadership-professional-de-

velopment/leadership/inclusive-leaders

11   Brown, J. (2019). How to be an inclusive leader: Your role in creating cultures of belonging where everyone can thrive.

12   Sweeney, C., & Bothwick, F. (2016). Inclusive leadership: The definitive guide to developing and executing an impactful diversity and inclusion strategy - locally and globally.

13   https://www2.deloitte.com/content/dam/Deloitte/us/Documents/about-deloitte/us-incl-six-signature-traits-inclusive-leadership.pdf

14   https://www2.deloitte.com/content/dam/Deloitte/us/Documents/about-deloitte/us-incl-six-signature-traits-inclusive-leadership.pdf

15   https://www.kornferry.com/capabilities/leadership-professional-development/leadership/inclusive-leaders

16   https://www.kornferry.com/capabilities/leadership-professional-development/leadership/inclusive-leaders

17   https://www.kornferry.com/insights/featured-topics/diversity-equity-inclusion/guide-to-dei-in-the-workplace

18   Sundiatu Dixon-Fyle, Kevin Dolan, Vivian Hunt, and Sara Prince, Diversity Wins: How Inclusion Matters (McKinsey & Company, May 19, 2020).

19   Credit Suisse (2016). Credit Suisse ESG Research. https://plus.credit-suisse.com/rpc4/ravDocView?docid=QYuHK2

20   https://www.accenture.com/t20181108T081959Z__w__/us-en/_acnmedia/PDF-89/Accenture-Disability-Inclusion-Research-Report.pdf

21   https://www.kornferry.com/insights/featured-topics/diversity-equity-inclusion/guide-to-dei-in-the-workplace

22   Steven A. Creek, Kristine M. Kuhn, and Arvin Sahaym, Board Diversity and Employee Satisfaction: The Mediating Role of Progressive Programs, Group & Organization Management (2017).

23 Jie Chen, Woon Sau Leung, Wei Song, and Marc Georgen, Research: When Women Are on Boards, Male CEOs Are Less Overconfident, Harvard Business Review, September 12, 2019; Jie Chen, Woon Sau Leung, Wei Song, and Marc Georgen, Why Female Board Representation Matters: The Role of Female Directors in Reducing Male CEO Overconfidence, Journal of Empirical Finance, vol. 52 (2019): p. 70-90.

24 Yaoyao Fan, Yuxiang Jiang, Xuezhi Zhang, and Yue Zhou, Women on Boards and Bank Earnings Management: From Zero to Hero, Journal of Banking & Finance, vol. 107 (2019).

25 Binay K. Adhikari, Anup Agrawal, and James Malm, Do Women Managers Keep Firms Out of Trouble? Evidence from Corporate Litigation and Policies, Journal of Accounting and Economics, vol. 67, no. 1 (2019): p. 202-225.

26 Paula Loop and Paul DeNicola, You've Committed to Increasing Gender Diversity on Your Board. Here's How to Make It Happen, Harvard Business Review, February 18, 2019.

27 https://www.forbes.com/sites/forbesinsights/2020/01/15/diversity-confirmed-to-boost-innovation-and-financial-results/

28 International Labour Organization, Women in Business and Management: The Business Case for Change (2019): p. 21.

29 https://www.kornferry.com/insights/featured-topics/diversity-equity-inclusion/guide-to-dei-in-the-workplace

30 https://www.kornferry.com/insights/featured-topics/diversity-equity-inclusion/guide-to-dei-in-the-workplace

31 Rocío Lorenzo, Nicole Voigt, Karin Schetelig, Annika Zawadzki, Isabell M. Welpe, and Prisca Brosi, The Mix That Matters: Innovation Through Diversity (The Boston Consulting Group, 2017).

32 Helen H. Yu and David Lee, Gender and Public Organization: A Quasi-Experimental Examination of Inclusion on Experiencing and Reporting Wrongful Behavior in the Workplace, Public Personnel

Management, vol. 49, no. 1 (2020): p. 3-28.

33 Juliet Bourke and Andrea Espedido, Why Inclusive Leaders Are Good for Organizations, and How to Become One, Harvard Business Review, March 29, 2019.

34 The Business Case for Diversity in the Workplace: sexual orientation and gender identity Report on good practices, European Commission: https://www.raznolikost.hr/admin/uploads/trainers/report_companies_final_en.pdf

35 https://www.dol.gov/

36 https://www.business.com/articles/hire-disabled-people/

37 https://economictimes.indiatimes.com/news/company/corporate-trends/what-companies-and-government-are-doing-to-empower-persons-with-disabilities/articleshow/65254315.cms?-from=mdr

38 https://www.ey.com/en_cn/forensic-integrity-services/how-to-get-the-benefits-of-a-neurodiverse-workforce

39 Adichie, C. N. (2015). We should all be feminists.

40 https://www.nytimes.com/2022/06/01/technology/elon-musk-tesla-spacex-office.html

41 https://www.uschamber.com/co/run/human-resources/companies-offering-flexible-work-schedules

42 https://fortune.com/2022/03/21/9-to-5-dead-flexible-schedules-more-popular/

43 https://futureforum.com/pulse-survey/

44 https://www.cnbc.com/2022/04/20/how-flexible-work-arrangements-can-help-companies-become-more-diverse-and-inclusive.html

45 https://www.crayola.com/product-feature/colors-of-the-world

46 www.nike.com

47 https://ankhgear.com/collections/apparel

48 Luthra, P. (2021). Diversifying Diversity: Your Guide to Being an Active Ally of Inclusion in the Workplace. Diversifying Diversity ApS.

49 https://www.forbes.com/sites/daviddisalvo/2013/06/22/your-brain-sees-even-when-you-dont/

50 Libet, B. (1985). Unconscious Cerebral Initiative and the Role of Conscious Will in Voluntary Action. Behavioral and Brain Sciences, 8(4), 529–566

51 https://www.princeton.edu/news/2006/08/22/snap-judgments-decide-faces-character-psychologist-finds

52 https://theglasshammer.com/2017/01/takes-seven-seconds-make-good-first-impression/

53 Coca-Cola's anti-prejudice Middle East campaign "No labels this Ramadan": https://youtu.be/84OT0NLlqfM

54 https://www.kornferry.com/insights/this-week-in-leadership/job-interview-first-impressions

55 https://implicit.harvard.edu/implicit/takeatest.html

56 https://qz.com/794740/the-happiness-of-the-danes-can-easily-be-explained-by-10-cultural-rules/

57 McIntosh, P. (2003). White privilege: Unpacking the invisible knapsack. In S. Plous (Ed.), Understanding prejudice and discrimination (p. 191–196). McGraw-Hill.

58 Luthra, P. (2021). Diversifying Diversity: Your Guide to Being an Active Ally of Inclusion in the Workplace. Diversifying Diversity ApS.

59 Jones, K. P., Peddie, C. I., Gilrane, V. L., King, E. B., & Gray, A. L. (2016). Not So Subtle: A Meta-Analytic Investigation of the Correlates of Subtle and Overt Discrimination. Journal of Management, 42(6), 1588–1613.

60 https://hbr.org/2022/03/we-need-to-retire-the-term-microaggressions

61 https://hbr.org/2022/03/we-need-to-retire-the-term-microaggressions

62 https://www.bbc.com/news/uk-53425148

63 2014 study by George Washington University: https://www.research-gate.net/publication/275005639_Influence_of_Communication_Partner's_Gender_on_Language

64 https://hbr-org.cdn.ampproject.org/c/s/hbr.org/amp/2020/11/what-inclusive-leaders-sounds-like

65 https://amycedmondson.com/

66 https://metro-co-uk.cdn.ampproject.org/c/s/metro.co.uk/2020/09/25/black-and-ethnic-minority-employees-need-more-mental-health-support-in-the-workplace-13325119/amp/

67 https://www.merriam-webster.com/dictionary/gaslighting

68 https://www.monster.com/

69 Stern, R. (2007). The gaslight effect: How to spot and survive the hidden manipulations other people use to control your life. New York: Morgan Road Books.

70 Edmondson, Amy. (1999). Psychological safety and learning behavior in teams. Administrative Science Quarterly. 44. 250-282.

71 Brown, B. (2013). DARING GREATLY: How the Courage to Be Vulnerable Transforms the Way We Live, Love, Parent and Lead. London, England: Portfolio Penguin.

72 https://youtu.be/m1tTZSuHJKM

73 https://www.youtube.com/watch?v=fl5xurWyV2o

74 https://hbr.org/2021/06/dont-just-mentor-women-and-people-of-color-sponsor-them

75 https://hbr.org/2021/06/dont-just-mentor-women-and-people-of-color-sponsor-them

76 https://www.wsj.com/articles/how-godivas-choco-

late-chief-was-molded-11595649626

77   https://hbr.org/2021/06/dont-just-mentor-women-and-people-of-color-sponsor-them

78   https://businesschief.com/leadership-and-strategy/what-should-you-look-mentor

79   https://www.peoplemattersglobal.com/news/leadership/whom-does-leena-nair-turn-to-when-in-self-doubt-indra-nooyi-31959